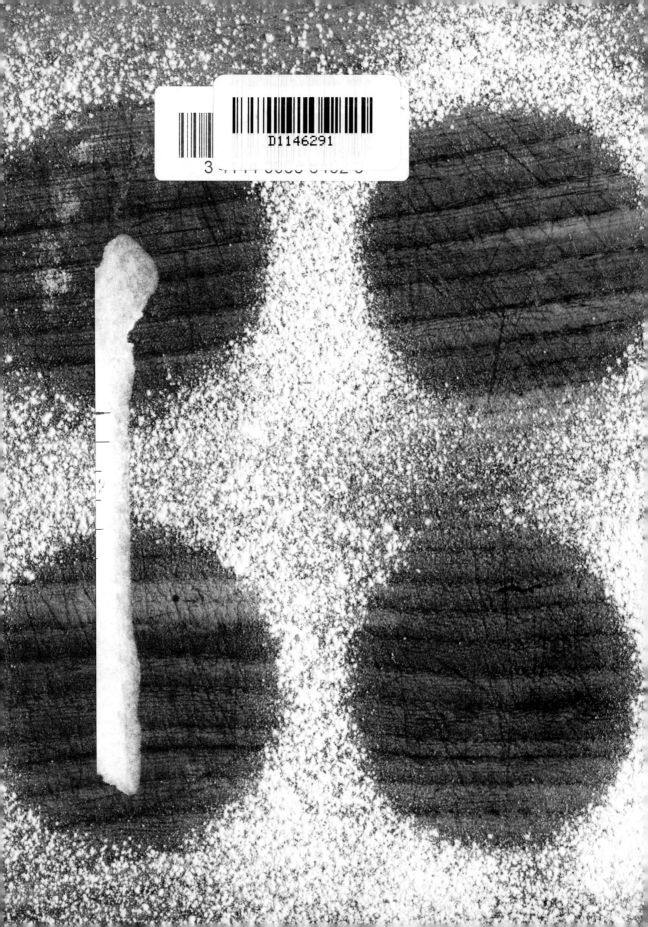

Sweet Things
From the Aga

Right: **Chocolate Peanut Butter Pie, page 144**

HANNAH MILES

Sweet Things

FROM THE AGA

A.

First published in Great Britain in 2013 by
Absolute Press, an imprint of
Bloomsbury Publishing Plc

Absolute Press
Scarborough House
29 James Street West
Bath BA1 2BT
Phone 44 (0) 1225 316013
Fax 44 (0) 1225 445836
E-mail info@absolutepress.co.uk
Website www.absolutepress.co.uk

Publisher Jon Croft
Commissioning Editor Meg Avent
Art Director Matt Inwood
Project Editor Alice Gibbs
Editor Eleanor Zandt
Photographer Mike Cooper
Food Stylist Hannah Miles

ISBN: 9781906650834

Printed in China by South China Printing
Company, Dongguan, Guangdong

A note about the text
This book is set in Sabon MT and Edwardian
Script. Sabon was designed by Jan Tschichold in
1964. The roman design is based on type by
Claude Garamond, whereas the italic design is
based on types by Robert Granjon. Edwardian
Script was designed by Edward Benguiat,
who gave his font the look of the writing of a
steel-point pen.

Bloomsbury Publishing
50 Bedford Square, London WC1B 3DP
www.bloomsbury.com

Acknowledgements
With heartfelt thanks to Jon, Meg and Matt at
Absolute Press for allowing me to write a book
about my beloved Aga and for producing it so
beautifully. Eleanor – much love and thanks for
your patient editing, it was a joy to work with
you. Special thanks to Mike Cooper for all the
beautiful photos – your visits to my cottage
were truly special. To Liam and Mark, many
thanks for all your hard work at the photography
shoots – it was definitely not the same when you
weren't there! My Mum, for all your help at the
photography shoots, particularly making such
fine choux pastry – I love you. Jess, Pam and
Vickie with your wonderful tidying and
cleaning skills, my Aga has never shone so
brightly before! Kathy Brown – for violet tea
and chats when I couldn't see the wood for
the trees and for getting me back on track.
Heather, Ellie and Claire at HHB Agency –
for being such wonderful and supportive friends
over the past five years. Elizabeth of Mar – for
publicising this book. My dad and brother – for
always being there – you are the best. My recipe
tasters – Kathy, Margaret, Maren, Tina, Josh,
Rosie, Miles, Charles, Nic, Al, Lucy, David,
Jennifer, Steven, Alison, Darren, Ella, Torin,
Pauline, Barbara, Millie, Andrew, Zara, Lauren,
Peter, Susan, Liz and Mike, and to Tena, who
passed her Aga on to me when I moved into
her cottage.

Contents

*W*hen I moved into my cottage eight years ago and was confronted by a cream-coloured Aga nestling in the kitchen, a friend told me that once I had cooked on an Aga I wouldn't be able to live without it.

At the time, I wasn't convinced; after all, it was just another type of oven, wasn't it? How wrong I was! Eight years later, the Aga is very much the centre of my home: it dries the washing; my cats, Muffy and Peapod, lie curled up in front of it to get warm; it dries wellington boots after long country walks; and most of all, it cooks delicious food. Over the last few years I have cooked on several different Agas, and no two are the same. My own Aga (which is fairly old) can be somewhat temperamental – it doesn't like windy weather and the hot spots can vary from day to day – but I love it all the same. Cooking with an Aga is much less about cooking by temperature and timing and more about cooking by sight, feel and instinct. Although this may seem daunting initially, with a little practice you will learn how your Aga works.

The Aga has no air circulation inside. The upside to this is that you can cook a curry and a cake in the oven at the same time and the flavour of the spices won't transfer to the cake. The downside is that you can't smell anything outside the oven; and like many other Aga owners, I'm sure, I have occasionally left something in the Aga and completely forgotten about it, only to find the charred remains a few hours later. I solve this problem by using a kitchen timer on a ribbon around my neck so that I don't forget that there is something cooking!

At the time when I appeared on *MasterChef*, a few years ago, my Aga was my only cooker at home, and I found it very hard cooking in a regular oven again. The dishes I love to cook are mainly cooked very slowly in the Simmering Oven, and trying to do these in a one-hour time slot on the programme was very difficult. I remember judge John Torode shouting at me one day that I needed to stop cooking in a regular oven as if it were an Aga. You can take the girl away from the Aga but you can't take the Aga instinct out of the girl!

I always feel so sad in the summer when it is too hot to keep the Aga turned on (my bed is directly above the Aga – perfect in winter but not ideal when it is hot outside). Somehow the kitchen doesn't feel the same when it is off; the kitchen floor isn't warm and washing doesn't dry! For me, one of the best things about the Aga is that it is always ready to cook – there is no need to preheat the ovens and it makes a lot of cooking processes, such as proving dough and melting chocolate, so much easier.

If you haven't gathered it already, I love my Aga. The recipes in this book are things that I like baking most in it and I hope you enjoy them too.

Hannah x

YPES OF AGA

There are several different types of Aga. The first difference between them is fuel: they can be powered by oil, gas, solid fuel or electricity. However, the general cooking principles of the Aga are the same, no matter how it is fuelled (although with some of the modern electric ovens you have the luxury of being able to vary the temperature). Each has a burner in the bottom which heats the Aga's ovens to differing temperatures, depending on their location. The other main difference is the number of ovens an Aga contains. Until recently there were three basic models, containing 2 ovens, 3 ovens and 4 ovens. Now Aga has just released a brand–new 5-oven Aga. I must confess to being slightly covetous of this new model, but my 2-oven Aga copes fine with the large amount of cooking I do.

2-oven Aga

This model is relatively small and compact, and although it has less total oven space than the larger models, it is perfect for everyday family cooking. I have even managed to cook harvest supper for 80 people on my 2-oven Aga. In a 2-oven Aga, the top oven is the Roasting Oven, which Aga say should generally be around 240°C (+/- 10°) and which is perfect for roasting meats and vegetables, starting casseroles and other one-pot dishes, and cooking Yorkshire puddings. By inserting a cold plain shelf (see page 9) into the Roasting Oven, you can reduce the temperature below the shelf to about 180/190°C , making it suitable for baking cakes and pastries, which require a more gentle heat. The floor of the Roasting Oven is perfect for baking pizzas and boiling jams and chutneys.

The lower oven on a 2-oven Aga is the Simmering Oven, which has a low temperature (Aga say this should be about 120°C (+/- 10°). It is ideal for slow-cooking casseroles and for making porridge overnight and is the perfect temperature for meringues and pavlovas. Food does continue to cook in this oven, albeit slowly, so you need to take this into account if you transfer cooked food to the Simmering Oven to keep it warm.

On top of this Aga are two hotplates: a Boiling Plate (perfect for kettles and for boiling vegetables and other things that need rapid boiling) and a Simmering Plate, which is cooler and perfect for cooking pancakes and crumpets. You can fit several pans on to each plate, which is ideal when you have lots of things to cook.

3-oven Aga

In addition to the Roasting Oven and Simmering Oven, this model includes a Baking Oven, which has a temperature of 180°C (375°F) and is ideal for cooking cakes and biscuits and dishes that need a moderate temperature. The top includes the same hotplates as on a 2-oven Aga.

4-oven Aga

The fourth oven in this model is a Warming Oven, which is ideal for keeping food warm and for warming plates and serving dishes before meals. The top of this Aga also has a Warming Plate, perfect for keeping food and mugs of tea and coffee warm.

5-oven Aga

This model has the same ovens and hotplates as the 4-oven Aga, plus a Slow Cooking Oven, ideal for slow-cooked meats, casseroles, and stews and offering plenty of cooking space for large-scale entertaining.

COOKING TECHNIQUES

The key principles when cooking in an Aga are to keep checking what you are cooking and to control the temperature using cold shelves (see page 9) if your dish is cooking too quickly. Unlike a conventional oven, the temperature in the Aga will not drop noticeably when you open the Aga door and therefore you don't risk having a sponge cake, for example, sink if you open the door. If a cake or dish is browning too quickly, either place a cold shelf on top or transfer the food to a cooler oven and cook it for a longer period of time.

The actual cooking time will depend on how hot your Aga is. My Aga's Roasting Oven ranges generally between 230°C and 240°C. I find an oven thermometer (which is inexpensive) very useful for checking the actual temperature of the oven.

With my Aga, the side of the dish or pan nearest the burner is hotter than the other side. Therefore one side of my cake or dessert generally cooks more quickly than the other. In order to ensure even cooking, I turn my trays halfway through cooking, and you may find this useful if your Aga is similar to mine.

Always check that the item is cooked properly before removing it from the oven, even if the cooking time stated in the recipe has elapsed. Biscuits should be quite soft to the touch, as they will set once cool. Cakes should should spring back when pressed with a clean finger. You can also insert a sharp knife or skewer into the centre of a cake to test if it is done. If it comes out clean with no cake batter on it, the cake is ready. If there is still some sticky cake batter visible, the cake requires a little more cooking. The cooking times given in the recipes in this book are guidelines only; the actual cooking times will depend on the temperature of your Aga.

To ensure recipe success:
1) Read the whole recipe through first, before getting started.
2) Make sure that you follow each step of the recipe in the order given.
3) Measure the ingredients carefully. You may want to do this in advance of starting, as this will ensure that you use all the ingredients and don't miss any out and that you have everything you need. It is maddening to get halfway through a recipe and realise that you are missing a vital ingredient.

Proving
The warmth of the Aga is ideal for proving yeast doughs. Simply place your dough in a greased bowl covered with cling film and leave it on the front edge of the Aga or on a trivet placed on top of the Simmering Plate. Your dough will be doubled in size in no time at all.

Knocking back
This technique is used after the first proving to knock the excess air out of bread dough; you simply punch and knead the dough, reducing it in size, then leave to prove again before baking it.

Sterilising jars and bottles
To sterilise preserving jars and glass bottles in the Aga, wash the jars in hot soapy water and then rinse with clean water and wipe dry using a clean tea towel. Place the jars or bottles in a roasting pan and heat in the Simmering Oven for about 30 minutes. Take care when removing them from the oven as the glass will be hot.

Greasing and lining cake tins
When baking using tins or baking sheets you need to ensure that they are properly greased so that the cakes or cookies do not stick during cooking. Grease the tin or sheet using a little softened butter or a cake tin spray such as Bake Easy. Cut the baking parchment to the size needed and press it firmly into the tin. When lining a square tin, snip diagonal cuts at the edges so that the paper folds over neatly at the corners. When lining a round tin, cut out a circle of baking parchment slightly larger than the base of your tin and cut little snips, about 1–2cm apart, around the edge. This is most easily done with the paper folded into quarters. Place in the tin so that the cut edge comes up the sides of the tin. Cut a long strip of paper the height of the tin sides and long enough to go all the way round the tin. Place this in the greased tin, smoothing it so that it covers the snipped edge of the bottom piece.

Melting chocolate

When melting chocolate you need to ensure that all the equipment you use is dry, as water can affect its melting properties. Cut the chocolate into pieces and place it in a heatproof bowl, then simply leave it for about 10–15 minutes on top of the Aga. Stir to melt any remaining lumps of chocolate. If you are making chocolate ganache you add the butter and cream to the bowl once the chocolate is completely melted, and melt these ingredients in the same way.

Caramelising sugar

When caramelising sugar, use a clean, dry pan. Pour in the sugar and heat on the Boiling Plate. Do not stir the sugar but shake the pan from time to time to prevent it from sugar burning – indicated by its turning very dark brown and starting to smoke. Watch very closely towards the end of cooking, as the caramel can burn very quickly. You need to remember that the caramel will keep cooking in the hot pan, even after it is removed from the Boiling Plate, because the sides and base of the pan are hot, so you should remove it from the heat just before the caramel is ready. If you are using the caramel for sugar work, allow it to thicken for a minute or so before using it. If the caramel sets before you have finished your sugar work, simply return the pan to the Boiling Plate for a few seconds to melt the sugar again.

Whipping to soft/stiff peaks

Whipping cream or egg whites to peaks is best done with an electric stand mixer or electric whisk, as it takes a lot longer with a hand whisk, particularly in the case of egg whites. Place the cream or egg whites in a clean, dry bowl and whisk until the cream or egg whites stands in peaks when you lift up the beaters. For soft peaks the mixture should hold its shape but just flop over slightly. Stiff peaks look exactly as the term suggests. Take particular care when whipping cream, for if you over-whip, it will curdle and turn to butter. You may find it helpful first to place the bowl and beaters in the refrigerator for about 10–15 minutes, so that they, as well as the cream, are chilled.

Preparing buttercream

To make good buttercream, which is perfect for piping decorations, you need to whip in lots of air, so that the icing is light and creamy. For enough buttercream to cover 12 large cupcakes, sift 225g of icing sugar into a large mixing bowl and add 125g of butter. The butter must be very soft, otherwise you will end up with lumps in the icing. Add one tablespoon of milk and a little vanilla extract and whisk using an electric hand or stand mixer for about 2–3 minutes until the icing is very light; add a little more milk if the mixture is too dry. Spoon into a piping bag fitted with a nozzle of your choice and you are ready to start decorating.

BAKING EQUIPMENT

To make the recipes in this book you will need relatively few pieces of baking equipment, most of which you will probably have already in your own kitchen. There are some other items which – although involving some additional expenditure – really do help with baking and are a worthwhile investment; these include silicone mats and Bake-O-Glide, which are quite simply brilliant for cooking biscuits, macarons and meringues on as well as for lining the Boiling and Simmering Plates when cooking directly on the heat. Each recipe in this book states which special equipment is needed for the recipe, and it is important to check that you have everything a recipe calls for before starting to bake.

Cold plain shelves

For convenience called simply 'cold shelves', these are absolutely essential for cooking in the Aga, as they are your main method of controlling temperature and so ensuring that you don't burn your cakes and other baked goodies. They are also perfect for baking cookies and meringues on instead of a baking tray. I have three shelves and find that this is plenty.

Tins/Pans

A variety of tins and pans are used in the recipes in this book. It is worth investing in good-quality pans that will not rust or lose shape over time. I find that thinner pans can become warped in the Aga (this is particularly true of baking sheets) and this can affect your baking. It is worth investing in some of Aga's own good-quality bakeware. Their Cake Baker pan is especially useful; this is a cake tin enclosed in a metal container which helps to regulate the temperature and cook perfect cakes. Loose-bottomed tins have a base that can be lifted out, which makes it easy to remove the cake; a special kind of tin, called a 'springform tin', has tight-fitting sides that are loosened by means of a latch, releasing the cake. If you do not have the tin called for in a recipe you can use a similar-sized tin; but be aware that the baking time may need to be adjusted. For example, using a smaller tin than stipulated in the recipe but with the same quantity of cake batter will require a longer baking time, as the cake batter will be deeper in the tin.

Silicone mats/Bake-O-Glide
If you bake a lot then you may wish to consider investing in silicone mats. They are my 'can't live without' baking accessories: thin mats, made of silicone rubber, which you can cook on without greasing. Nothing sticks to them, so they are ideal for baking cookies and meringues. Bake-O-Glide is a thinner silicone sheet and is ideal when cooking directly on the hot plates. Although you can cook directly on the Aga hotplates, if your Aga, like mine, is rather old, the use of a mat is advisable.

Silicone cake moulds
A large variety of silicone moulds are available. These moulds can be baked in the Aga and come in decorative patterns and shapes.

Mixing equipment
For some of the recipes in this book, ingredients can be mixed with only a spoon, but most require the use of some special mixing equipment. A simple balloon whisk, used by hand, is useful for recipes that don't need much whipping, but whisking cake batters and cream is much quicker using an electric mixer. Although a hand-held electric mixer will suffice in most cases, a stand mixer will do all the mixing for you; for breads, such as brioche, a stand mixer fitted with a dough hook is highly recommended. Mixing jobs that also involve chopping or solid ingredients require a food processor.

Wire rack
Once biscuits and cakes are baked, you need, usually, to cool them on a wire rack. If they stay in the hot tin or on the baking sheet on which they were cooked, this can lead to overcooking – although some, such as brownies, do need to remain in the tin for awhile in order to set. Specific instructions for cooling are provided with the individual recipes. I often use my Aga

toast basket as an extra wire rack, as it is easily to hand, hanging on the side of the Aga.

Scales
Baking is a scientific process and for best results it is important that ingredients be weighed and measured carefully. Kitchen scales are therefore an essential part of your baking equipment kit. For the most accurate results use electronic scales.

Sugar thermometer
A sugar thermometer is essential when working with hot liquid ingredients that must be brought to a specific temperature, as in the recipe for Baked Alaska on page 152.

Blowtorch
You can use a chef's blowtorch to caramelise sugar and meringue. Unfortunately, because the Aga does not really have the ability to grill food, a blowtorch is essential for recipes such as the Ginger Brulées on page 133.

Piping (icing) bag and nozzles
For effective, neat decoration when icing a cake, you should use a piping bag with nozzle attachments. They are also useful for preparing choux buns and éclairs. Nozzles come in many different shapes and sizes, allowing you to be creative when decorating. The best way to learn how to use a piping bag and nozzle is to make a large batch of buttercream or royal icing and pipe different shapes using each nozzle to see what results you can achieve. Piping bags are available in different forms, including waterproof fabric bags, which will last a long time, and disposable plastic bags that are used just once. If you are using several different colours of icing it is easiest to use disposable bags, as a fabric bag will need to be washed and dried thoroughly between each use. Alternatively you can make your own piping bags using greaseproof paper or baking parchment folded into a paper cone.

Other items
You will also need a rolling pin, for rolling out pastry and some biscuits and breads; a pastry brush, for applying glazes; a spatula, for scraping mixtures out of mixing bowls and also for spooning them into piping bags; a palette knife, which has a rounded blade, for loosening set mixtures from moulds; a zester, for peeling little threads of citrus zest, and a trivet, on which to place some items on top of the Aga.

BASIC BAKING LARDER

Most of the recipes in this book are made with everyday store-cupboard ingredients such as flour, butter, sugar and eggs. Most baking ingredients have a long shelf life, so you can easily stock up on a basic larder, but make sure that ingredients have not reached their sell-by date before you use them, as products such as self-raising flour and baking powder can lose their raising properties over time. The main ingredients you will need are:

Syrups and sugars

Several varieties of syrup are used in this book, including golden syrup, honey, maple syrup, rose syrup and agave syrup. All add a delicious sweetness to cakes and other bakes. Black treacle is a strong-flavoured syrup that is used in gingerbreads.

Caster sugar is perfect for baking, as the crystals are small and so dissolve easily. It is the main sugar I use for baking and appears in many of the recipes in this book.

Granulated sugar has larger crystals than caster sugar. Although it can be substituted in recipes where sugar is melted, it will take a little longer to melt. As a general rule, better results are obtained when using caster sugar.

Brown sugars add a delicious caramel flavour to baked items due to their molasses content. These sugars are available in dark and light varieties, the colour depending on the quantity of molasses contained in the sugar. Dark brown sugar is best used in gingerbreads or rich cakes, whereas light brown sugar has a delicate caramel flavour and is delicious used in crumbles.

Muscovado sugar is an unrefined dark brown sugar which is slightly coarser and stickier than dark brown sugar and can be substituted for dark brown sugar in some recipes.

Icing sugar is a very fine powdered sugar that that can be dissolved in water to produce a runny icing which will set. It can be used to top cupcakes and to decorate cookies and can be coloured with food colouring pastes or gels for pretty effects, and it is also often simply sprinkled over the surface of baked items. Special kinds of icing sugar are used to make fondant and royal icing.

Flours and raising agents

Flours and raising agents are essential for almost all baking recipes and come in several varieties. For people who suffer from gluten intolerance, gluten-free flours and raising agents are available. Yeast is a raising agent commonly used in dough, especially for breads. It comes in fresh, dried and fast-action (similar to dried) varieties. Supermarkets with in-store bakeries will often give you a small quantity of fresh yeast free of charge.

Plain flour does not contain any raising agent and is used to make biscuits, bars and slices that do not need to rise. Always make sure you sift all flours before using to remove any lumps.

Strong flour has a higher gluten content than plain flour and so is especially suitable for making bread.

Wholemeal flour uses 100 per cent of the wheat grain – whereas plain flour uses only the white, starchy part – and so has more fibre.

Self-raising flour contains baking powder and is used to make cakes and chewy cookies. If you do not have self-raising flour available, you can add 5ml (1 teaspoon) baking powder to every 115g plain flour, sifting them together to make sure they are well mixed.

Baking powder is a powdered chemical raising agent made from two parts acidic cream of tartar and one part bicarbonate of soda. When mixed with liquids and heated, it releases air bubbles which cause baked goods to rise.

Bicarbonate of soda is a salty chemical agent which is often added to biscuits and muffins to give them a light and airy texture. It has a salty, soapy taste and should be used only sparingly.

Eggs

The recipes in this book use large eggs unless stated otherwise. Always use fresh eggs and wherever possible free-range or organic varieties, as their golden yolks give cakes and cookies a wonderful colour.

Dairy

When it comes to butter, it is preferable to use unsalted butter in the recipes, but you can substitute salted butter, omitting any salt added in the recipe, if you prefer. It is also possible to use margarine or other spreads which are suitable for baking in cake recipes, although in my view they don't give quite as nice a taste as butter. You should always use butter in biscuit recipes.

Some recipes in this book use mascarpone cheese: a thick Italian cream cheese which has a delicious rich flavour. Cream cheese is also used for cheesecakes. You can substitute low-fat cream cheese or low-fat mascarpone if you prefer.

Double cream is a thick cream which can be whipped to stiff peaks and is a delicious filling in cakes and meringues. You need to take care not to over-whip it when whisking, as it can curdle and become lumpy.

Clotted cream is a very thick set cream made by heating unpasteurised cow's milk. It has a buttery crust and is perfect with scones and jam. You can make your own in the Aga following the recipe on page 61.

Soured cream is a thick set cream with a slightly sour taste that can be added to cake batters or butter creams. If you do not have soured cream available you can make your own by adding about 1 tablespoon of lemon juice to 250ml double cream, stirring until the cream becomes thicker.

Crème fraîche is a French set cream which can be substituted for soured cream in many recipes. It is also delicious served as an accompaniment to cakes and desserts.

Buttermilk is the residue left when butter is churned. It has a slightly sour, acidic taste and is often used for making scones, for example.

Yoghurt is made from fermented milk. With its slightly sour taste, it can be used in the same way as soured cream to moisten cakes and to flavour butter icing. Both plain and Greek yoghurts are used in this book.

FLAVOURINGS

Both the juice and the zest of some citrus fruits can give a zingy flavour to cakes and cookies; limes, lemons, oranges and tangerines all work well. The juice can be heated and drizzled over just-baked sponges and the zest can be added to cake batter and cookie dough. Use a fine zester or grater, and make sure that you do not include the fruit's white pith, as this can give a bitter taste. Always make sure to remove any pips from the juice before using it.

A small quantity of freshly ground spice will transform the flavour of a recipe. Make sure that you use fresh spices and not ones that have passed their use-by date, as they lose strength of flavour over time.

Vanilla seeds from a vanilla pod give the best vanilla flavour but the pods are very expensive and so I tend to use a good-quality vanilla extract or vanilla bean paste for baking.

Chocolate chips can be added to cakes and cookies for extra texture and taste, and chocolate curls and chocolate-covered coffee beans are ideal cake decorations.

Many recipes in this book use nuts, in both whole and/or ground form. Take care when serving nuts, as some people suffer from nut allergies.

Sultanas, glacé cherries, dried cranberries and sour cherries are just some of the delicious dried fruits available which add flavour and texture to both cakes and cookies.

Coconut is available in many forms: fresh coconut (which you grate yourself), desiccated, long shredded soft coconut and flaked coconut strips. My preferred type of coconut for cake decorating and baking is long shredded soft coconut, as it gives a very pretty effect when coloured and tastes delicious.

Start of the Day

Ricotta pancakes with maple butter
makes 8

There are few better ways to start the day than with a stack of pancakes drizzled with maple syrup. The Simmering Plate of the Aga is perfect for cooking pancakes. You can either cook them directly on the plate – first well cleaned and greased with a little butter – or, as I do, cook them on a sheet of greased Bake-O-Glide placed directly on top of the Simmering Plate. For an extra treat, serve these breakfast pancakes with whipped maple butter – the perfect start to a weekend.

PREPARATION: 10 MINUTES | COOKING: 20 MINUTES

for the pancakes
170g self-raising flour, sifted
1 teaspoon baking powder
1 egg, separated
60g ricotta cheese
1 teaspoon vanilla extract
1 tablespoon caster sugar
200–250ml milk
butter for greasing, melted

for the maple butter
50ml maple syrup
85g butter, softened

maple syrup, to serve

equipment
sheet of Bake-O-Glide

Place the flour, baking powder, egg yolk, ricotta cheese, vanilla, caster sugar and 200ml milk in a mixing bowl and whisk together to a smooth batter using a hand whisk. Add the remaining milk gradually until the batter has a smooth dropping consistency. (You may not need all of the milk.)

In a separate bowl, whisk the egg white to stiff peaks using a mixer or hand whisk, then fold into the batter.

Place a sheet of Bake-O-Glide on the Simmering Plate and brush it with a little melted butter. Place small ladlefuls of batter on the sheet (about 3 at a time) and cook until the underside of each pancake is golden brown and the top is just cooked with a few bubbles starting to appear. This will take about 3 minutes. Turn the pancakes over using a spatula and cook on the other side until golden brown. Keep the pancakes warm in the Simmering Oven while you cook the remaining pancakes.

For the maple butter, whisk together the maple syrup and butter using an electric whisk until light and creamy. This is best made shortly before serving, for if you store it in the refrigerator the butter will set and lose its whipped texture. Serve the pancakes with the maple butter and a jug of maple syrup on the side.

Breakfast granola
makes approximately 800g / 2 large jars

Making granola at home is simple, and it makes a delicious breakfast served with natural yoghurt and a drizzle of honey. Once you have mastered the basic process, you can vary the recipe by adding different nuts and fruits. Do not be alarmed by the long list of ingredients – all you need to do is to stir them together and bake them slowly in the Simmering Oven. Packaged in preserving jars, labelled and tied with pretty ribbons, this granola makes a perfect hostess gift. To make this recipe gluten free, replace the flour with gluten-free self-raising flour and use gluten-free oats.

PREPARATION: 15 MINUTES | BAKING: ABOUT 1 HOUR

300g jumbo oats
100g sunflower seeds
80g flaked almonds
2 tablespoons sesame seeds
2 teaspoons ground cinnamon
1 teaspoon vanilla extract
1 tablespoon self-raising flour
60g light muscovado sugar
80ml maple syrup
80ml honey
2 tablespoons vegetable oil
100g dried cherries
100g dried blueberries

equipment
large Aga roasting pan, lined (see page 8)

Mix together the oats, sunflower seeds, flaked almonds and sesame seeds. Sprinkle the cinnamon, vanilla, flour and sugar on top (making sure that any lumps in the sugar are broken down).

Whisk together the maple syrup, honey and oil and pour this over the dry ingredients. Stir everything well so that all the dry ingredients are lightly coated with the syrup mixture.

Spread the mixture out on the roasting pan and bake on the bottom runners of the Roasting Oven for about 5 minutes until golden brown, stirring halfway through cooking. Take care that the mixture doesn't brown too much, covering it with a cold shelf if it does. Transfer it to the middle runners of the Simmering Oven and bake for about 1 hour until the mixture is crisp and golden.

Leave the granola to cool, then stir through the dried cherries and blueberries. Store it in sterilised, airtight jars (see page 8) until you are ready to use it.

Apple and cinnamon porridge
serves 8

Porridge is one of my favourite things to make in the Aga. It takes only a few minutes to prepare before you go to bed, and then by morning it's deliciously creamy, even though it is made with water. The fruit makes it extra-healthy and sweet. You can eat this porridge as it is or, for a special treat, serve it with whipped cream or crème fraîche, drizzled with maple syrup.

PREPARATION: 5 MINUTES | COOKING: APPROXIMATELY 7–8 HOURS

150g pinhead oatmeal
1.2 litres water
2 small apples, cored and grated
2 teaspoons ground cinnamon
100g jumbo sultanas

equipment
heavy-based casserole dish with tight-fitting lid

Place all the ingredients in the pan and bring to the boil on the Boiling Plate. Remove from the heat, cover with the lid and place in the Simmering Oven overnight, for about 7–8 hours.

First thing in the morning, remove the porridge from the oven and stir well, adding a little hot water if it is too thick. Serve, if you like, with crème fraîche, or whipped cream, and maple syrup to drizzle.

You can make this with regular oats by following the heating instructions but rather than placing it in the Simmering Oven, leave the pan covered on the back of the Aga overnight instead.

Wholesome breakfast muffins

makes 8

These tasty muffins are packed with banana, apricots and prunes. Topped with a touch of granola and strawberry pieces, they are an ideal breakfast treat served hot from the Aga. If you do not have agave syrup you can substitute the same amount of runny, or clear, honey.

PREPARATION: 15 MINUTES | BAKING: 20–25 MINUTES

1 ripe banana
juice of $1/2$ lemon
115g butter, softened
40ml light agave syrup
2 eggs
60ml buttermilk
1 teaspoon vanilla extract
115g self-raising flour, sifted
1 teaspoon baking powder
2 ripe apricots, stoned and finely chopped
3 soft prunes, stoned and chopped
80g juicy sultanas
1 tablespoon freeze-dried strawberry pieces

for the topping
50g granola (shop-bought or see recipe, page 19)
1 tablespoon freeze-dried strawberry pieces

equipment
muffin tin lined with 8 muffin cases

Peel the banana and mash it to a smooth paste with the lemon juice using a fork. In a mixing bowl, whisk together the butter, mashed banana and syrup until smooth and creamy. Add the eggs and whisk again. Fold in the buttermilk, vanilla, self-raising flour and baking powder using a spatula. Stir through the chopped apricots and prunes, sultanas, and strawberry pieces.

Spoon the mixture into the muffin cases and sprinkle with the granola. Bake in the Roasting Oven below a cold shelf (or in the Baking Oven) for about 20–25 minutes, until the muffins are golden brown and spring back to your touch. Sprinkle the remaining strawberry pieces on top and leave to cool for a few minutes before serving.

The muffins can be stored in an airtight container for up to 3 days, but are best eaten on the day they are made.

Homemade crumpets
makes 10-12

Although you can buy crumpets in the supermarket, making them at home is easy to do on an Aga and the results are far superior. There is no nicer treat than eating them warm straight from the Aga, spread with lashings of butter and jam.

PREPARATION: 20 MINUTES | PROVING TIME: 45 MINUTES | COOKING: 20–30 MINUTES

1 tablespoon caster sugar
7g fast-action dried yeast
400ml milk, warmed
200ml water, warmed
340g strong flour
110g self-raising flour
$1/2$ teaspoon salt
butter for greasing, melted

equipment
four 9cm crumpet or chef's rings, Bake-O-Glide
   (optional)

Place the sugar and yeast in a jug with the warm milk and water. Leave for 5–10 minutes on top of the Aga until a thick foam forms on top of the liquid.

Sift the strong flour and self-raising flour into a large bowl and whisk in the salt and the yeast mixture. Cover the bowl with cling film and leave for about 45 minutes on top of the Aga until the mixture has doubled in size.

Grease the insides of the rings lightly with butter. Cover the Simmering Plate with a sheet of Bake-O-Glide and grease with a little butter; or grease the (clean) plate itself and cook directly on it. Place the crumpet rings on top of the Simmering Plate and pour a small ladleful of batter into each ring.

Leave the crumpets to cook for about 5 minutes, until holes start to form on top and they are almost cooked. Using oven gloves, remove the rings (slide a knife around the inside edge if needed) and turn the crumpets over using a spatula; cook until they are golden brown. Repeat the process, re-using the rings, until all the remaining batter is used.

These crumpets are best served warm, so eat them straight away. Or if you are serving them later, toast them before serving.

Brioche with apricot butter
makes 2 loaves

I am not going to lie to you – making brioche takes a long time and it contains an obscene amount of butter. When I was testing this recipe I grumbled to a friend that I couldn't see why anyone would want to spend so many hours on one recipe when you can buy delicious brioche loaves in the shops. However, when we had a slice straight from the Aga, we knew immediately that it was worth all the work. This brioche literally melts in the mouth, and spread with apricot butter, it is the most perfect treat for a special occasion. You really do need a stand mixer with a dough hook for this recipe; otherwise it gets messy when you add the butter and entails a lot of kneading.

PREPARATION: 25 MINUTES | PROVING: 4–5 HOURS | BAKING: 20–25 MINUTES

2 tablespoons warm water
7g fast-action dried yeast
70g caster sugar
500g strong white flour, sifted
6 eggs
375g butter, cut into small cubes

for the glaze
1 egg
1 tablespoon icing sugar

for the apricot butter
7 ripe apricots, halved and with stones removed
50g butter
30g caster sugar

equipment
2 brioche pans approximately 16cm in diameter, greased; Aga-proof dish; blender or food processor; stand mixer with a dough hook

Place the warm water in a jug with the yeast and 1 tablespoon of the caster sugar and leave on top of the Aga for about 10 minutes until a thick foam has formed on top of the water.

Place the flour and remaining sugar in the bowl of a stand mixer; pour in the yeast liquid and mix with a dough hook. Beat in the eggs one at a time until you have a smooth dough. Once all the eggs are added, mix the dough for a further 3 or so minutes until it is smooth and silky and comes away from the sides of the bowl. Add the butter piece by piece to the dough while still mixing, until all of it is incorporated and the dough is glossy and comes away from the sides of the bowl. Cover the bowl with lightly greased cling film and leave it to prove on top of the Aga for

3 hours or until the dough has doubled in size. Knock back the dough on a flour-dusted surface and knead again, then shape into 2 round loaves and place in the brioche pans.

Whisk together the egg and icing sugar for the glaze and brush over the dough with a pastry brush. You may not need all of the glaze. Cover each pan loosely with a layer of cling film and leave for 1–2 hours on top of the Aga until the loaves have doubled in size.

Bake the loaves on the bottom runners of the Roasting Oven for 20–30 minutes until they are golden brown, covering them with a cold shelf if they start to brown too much (or use the Baking Oven). Turn them once to ensure even cooking. Leave them to cool (although you may wish to eat a slice or two still warm from the Aga – scrumptious!).

For the apricot butter, place the halved apricots in an Aga-proof dish, sprinkle with the sugar and add the butter. Bake in the Simmering Oven for 1 hour until the fruit is soft, then purée in a food processor or blender to a smooth paste. Serve the apricot butter with thick slices of brioche, toasted if you like.

The brioche is best eaten on the day it is made, although it can be stored in an airtight container for up to 2 days. Alternatively, cut the loaf into slices and freeze in individual portions, then toast in an Aga basket.

Giant sweet and salty pretzels
makes 6

These pretzels are not the small crisp variety that are found in Britain but are the soft dough pretzels that are served in Germany, particularly at Christmas markets. Served warm, they are delicious eaten on their own or as an accompaniment to soup or goulash. Twisting the pretzels into their classic shape is not as difficult as it looks, although if you prefer you can simply form the dough into balls for pretzel rolls.

PREPARATION: 25 MINUTES | PROVING: 1 HOUR | BAKING: 10–15 MINUTES

7g fast-action dried yeast
30g caster sugar
80ml warm water in a jug
400g plain flour, plus extra for dusting
$1/2$ teaspoon salt
1 tablespoon butter, softened
200ml warm water

For the simmering solution
2 tablespoons bicarbonate of soda
salt flakes and sugar to sprinkle

Equipment
large baking sheet lined with a silicone mat;
    stand mixer with a dough hook (optional)

Sprinkle the dried yeast and caster sugar over the 80ml warm water. Leave in a jug on top of the Aga for 10 minutes until a thick foam has formed on the surface.

Sift the flour into a large bowl, and mix in the salt, butter and yeast mixture. Add about 200ml of warm water gradually until you have a soft but not sticky dough. You may not need all of the water. Knead the dough well for about 10 minutes using a stand mixer fitted with a dough hook, or knead it by hand, then place it in a lightly greased bowl and leave for 1 hour until it has doubled in size.

Divide the dough into 6 pieces and roll each piece into a long sausage shape. To shape each pretzel, cross the ends of the dough over each other, then twist again and press on to the top of the dough loop, as shown in the picture, securing the ends in place with a little water. Place the shaped pretzels on a baking sheet lined with a silicone mat.

To prepare the simmering solution, heat 2 litres of water with the bicarbonate of soda in a large pan on the Simmering Plate until hot, but not boiling. Using a slotted spoon, lower each pretzel into the water, one at a time, and leave to cook for 1 minute, then remove using the slotted spoon and return to the tray. Repeat with the remaining pretzels. It is this step that gives the pretzels their classic salty coating.

Sprinkle the pretzels with a little sugar and a few flakes of salt. Cut snips with sharp clean scissors into the top of the dough. Bake in the Roasting Oven on the bottom runners for 10-15 minutes (or in the Baking Oven) until they are golden brown, turning the tray halfway through cooking if needed.

These pretzels are best eaten straight from the oven and must be consumed on the day they are made, as they do not keep.

Sticky Chelsea buns
makes 12

After appearing on *MasterChef* I was lucky enough to work at Fitzbillies Bakery in Cambridge – famous especially for its Chelsea buns, which are shipped all over the world. Although their recipe remains a trade secret, I devised my own version, inspired by head baker Gill Abbs, who loves baking as much as I do.

PREPARATION: 30 MINUTES | PROVING: 45 MINUTES | BAKING: 20–25 MINUTES

200ml milk, warmed
7g fast-action dried yeast
2 tablespoons caster sugar
200g plain flour
160g self-raising flour
1 teaspoon salt
60g butter, plus extra for greasing
2 eggs, beaten
400g mincemeat
2 teaspoons ground cinnamon

for the syrup

3 tablespoons golden syrup
50g dark brown sugar
2 teaspoons cinnamon
1 tablespoon butter
1 teaspoon vanilla extract

equipment

38 x 28cm baking tin, greased

Place the warm milk, yeast, and sugar in a jug and whisk together. Leave on top of the Aga for about 10 minutes until a thick foam appears on top of the milk.

Sift both flours and the salt into a large mixing bowl and whisk in the butter and eggs. Add the milk mixture and bring together into a soft dough. Knead, using a stand mixer fitted with a dough hook, for 10 minutes until the dough is soft and pliable. If you do not have a stand mixer, knead the dough on a flour-dusted surface, pulling and pushing the dough with the base of your hands. Leave the dough to rest for 5 minutes, then roll it out into a rectangle about 40 x 30cm.

Spread the mincemeat over the dough and sprinkle the cinnamon on top. Roll up the dough, pulling as you roll to form a tight spiral. Cut the roll into 12 slices. Place the slices in a roasting pan, leaving a gap between each bun as they will spread during proving. Cover the tray with greased cling film and place on top of the Aga. Leave to prove for 45 minutes or until the dough has doubled in size.

Bake the buns for 20–25 minutes in the Roasting Oven (or the Baking Oven) until they are golden brown and sound hollow when you tap them. Use a cold shelf in the Roasting Oven if the buns start to brown too much.

Place the syrup ingredients in a saucepan along with 40ml of water, heat on the Simmering Plate until the butter has melted and sugar dissolved. Spoon the syrup over the warm buns while they are still warm and leave for the syrup to soak in.

These buns are best eaten on the day they are made.

Cinnamon swirl loaf
makes 2 small loaves

This loaf, with a delectable sweet cinnamon, buttery filling, is a perfect breakfast treat.
For maximum enjoyment serve it either warm, straight from the oven, or toasted.

PREPARATION: 20 MINUTES | PROVING: 1½ HOURS | BAKING: 20–25 MINUTES

7g fast-action dried yeast
3 tablespoons caster sugar
250ml milk, warmed
450g strong flour
1 egg
2 tablespoon butter, softened

for the filling
115g caster sugar
60g butter, softened
1 tablespoon ground cinnamon

for the glaze
1 egg
1 tablespoon caster sugar

equipment
two 22 x 8.5cm loaf pans, greased; stand mixer
   with a dough hook (optional)

Add the yeast and one tablespoon of the sugar to
the warm milk in a jug and leave on the top of
the Aga for about 10 minutes until a thick foam
has formed on top of the milk.

Sift the flour into a large mixing bowl; add the
remaining 2 tablespoons of sugar, the egg and
the butter. Pour in the milk mixture and mix
together to form a soft dough. Knead for about
10 minutes, either using a dough hook on a
stand mixer or by hand, until the dough is soft
and elastic.

Place the dough in a large greased bowl and
cover with cling film; leave on top of the Aga
for about an hour until the dough has doubled
in size. Knock the dough back (see page 8) to
remove the air and place it on a flour-dusted
surface. Roll it out into a rectangle about 30 x
20cm in size.

For the filling, mix together the caster sugar,
butter and cinnamon to a smooth paste. Spread
this over the rolled-out dough in a thin layer,
leaving about 2cm around each edge of the
dough with no filling. Roll the dough up from
one of the narrow ends pulling the dough as you
roll to form a tight spiral. Cut the dough in half
and place one half in each of the prepared pans.

For the glaze, whisk together the egg and caster
sugar and brush over the top of the loaves using
a pastry brush. You may not need all of the glaze.

Cover the pans in lightly greased cling film
and leave them on top of the Aga for a further
30 minutes or so until the loaves have doubled
in size.

Bake the loaves for 10 minutes in the Roasting
Oven, turning them after 5 minutes, then
cover with a cold shelf and bake for a further
10–15 minutes (or use the Baking Oven) until
the loaves are golden brown and sound hollow
when you tap them.

These loaves are best eaten on the day they
are made, but they freeze well cut into slices.
You can toast the slices straight from the freezer
in an Aga toast basket.

Teatime Treats

Banana shortbread
makes 14

These shortbreads are made with sun-dried bananas, which have a rich caramel banana flavour. They are available in health food shops, but if you have difficulty finding them you can substitute dried banana chips, for equally delicious results.

PREPARATION: 15 MINUTES | BAKING: 10–15 MINUTES | CHILLING: 1 HOUR

115g butter, softened
60g caster sugar
70g sun-dried bananas or dried banana chips
14 dried banana chips, for decoration
115g plain flour, plus extra for dusting
60g cornflour

equipment
2 baking trays, greased and lined; 9cm flower-
   shaped cutter

Whisk together the butter and sugar until light and creamy.

Blitz the dried bananas in a food processor to fine crumbs.

Sift the flour and cornflour into the butter mixture, add the banana crumbs and whisk together to a soft dough. Wrap the dough in cling film and chill in the refrigerator for an hour.

Remove the dough from the refrigerator and leave for 10 minutes until soft enough to roll out. Dust a clean work surface or silicone mat with flour and roll out the shortbread, using a rolling pin, to 5mm thickness. Cut out 14 shortbreads, re-rolling the dough as necessary, and transfer to the trays using a spatula. Press a banana chip into the top of each cookie.

Bake in the Roasting Oven below a cold shelf (or in the Baking Oven) for 10–15 minutes until golden brown, turning the trays halfway through cooking. Leave to cool on the trays for a few minutes, then transfer to a wire rack to cool.

These biscuits will keep for up to 5 days stored in an airtight container.

Sweet Things From the Aga

Gingerbread hearts
makes 12

At Christmas these ribbon-threaded hearts make pretty tree decorations. They can also be packaged up in bags tied with matching ribbon and presented as gifts. You can even hang them on a long ribbon to make festive gingerbread bunting.

PREPARATION: 15 MINUTES | CHILLING: 2 HOURS | BAKING: 8–12 MINUTES

70g butter
70g dark brown sugar
2 tablespoons golden syrup
1 tablespoon treacle
1 teaspoon vanilla extract
200g plain flour
1 teaspoon bicarbonate of soda
1 teaspoon ground ginger
1 teaspoon ground cinnamon

equipment
2 large baking trays, greased and lined; 8cm heart-shaped biscuit cutter; small round icing nozzle (5mm); narrow ribbon

Heat the butter, sugar, golden syrup, treacle and vanilla in a saucepan until the butter and sugar have melted. Leave to cool.

Sift the flour, bicarbonate of soda, ginger and cinnamon into a bowl. Pour in the syrup mixture and stir until all the flour is incorporated. The mixture will be quite sticky. Leave the mixture to cool and then chill in the refrigerator for 2 hours until it is firm.

On a flour-dusted work surface roll out the dough to 5mm thickness using a rolling pin. Cut out 12 heart shapes and place them about 4cm apart on the trays, as the biscuits will spread during baking. Bake on the bottom runners of the Roasting Oven under a cold shelf (or in the Baking Oven) for about 8–12 minutes.

Remove the biscuits from the oven, and while they are still warm, stamp out holes around the edge of the heart using the icing nozzle: 3 on each side of the heart. It is not possible to do this once the biscuits have cooled, as they would snap. Leave the biscuits to cool and then thread ribbon through the holes, tying it in a bow at the top of each heart.

These biscuits will keep for up to 5 days stored in an airtight container.

Cherry and coconut cookies
makes 24

These cookies are bursting with glacé cherries and coconut – one of my favourite flavour combinations. I use soft, long, shredded coconut, as it gives the cookies a great texture, but you can substitute desiccated coconut if you prefer.

PREPARATION: 15 MINUTES | BAKING: 10–15 MINUTES

125g butter
2 tablespoons golden syrup
350g self-raising flour
1 teaspoon bicarbonate of soda
200g caster sugar
100g long shredded sweet coconut (such as
   Baker's Angel Flake)
200g glacé cherries, halved
1 large egg, beaten

equipment
3 large baking trays lined with silicone mats or
   baking parchment

Heat the butter and syrup together until the butter has melted; leave to cool.

Sift the flour and bicarbonate of soda into a mixing bowl. Add the sugar, coconut and cherries, and stir in. Whisk the egg into the flour mixture. Pour in the syrup mixture and stir well so that all the ingredients are mixed and you have a soft cookie dough.

Place 24 mounds of dough, about a tablespoon in size, on the trays, placing them a distance apart, as the cookies will spread during cooking. Place the trays on the middle and bottom runners of the Roasting Oven and cover with a cold shelf (or use the Baking Oven) and bake for 10–15 minutes until golden brown, turning the trays halfway through cooking. The bottom trays will take a little longer.

Remove the trays from the oven, leave the cookies on the trays for 5 minutes so that they set, and then transfer to a wire rack using a spatula.

These cookies will keep for up to 5 days stored in an airtight container.

Orange and cranberry cookies
makes 24

I like the American term 'cookie' for the soft, chewy kind of biscuit. These cookies are made with a buttery syrup and are delicious. If you don't have dried cranberries in your cupboard, you can substitute sultanas or raisins for equally yummy cookies.

PREPARATION: 15 MINUTES | BAKING: 10–15 MINUTES

125g butter
2 tablespoons golden syrup
350g self-raising flour
1 teaspoon bicarbonate of soda
1 teaspoon ground cinnamon
pinch of salt
200g caster sugar
100g dried cranberries
zest of 1 large orange
1 large egg, beaten
100g milk chocolate chips

equipment
3 large baking trays lined with silicone mats or
   baking parchment

Heat the butter and syrup together until the butter has melted, then leave to cool.

Sift the flour, bicarbonate of soda, cinnamon and salt into a mixing bowl. Add the sugar, cranberries, orange zest and the egg. Pour in the cooled syrup mixture and whisk together until you have a soft dough. Add the chocolate chips and mix in.

Place 24 spoonfuls of the mixture on the trays, positioning them a small distance apart, as the cookies will spread while baking. Place the trays on the middle and bottom runners of the Roasting Oven below a cold shelf (or the Baking Oven) and bake the cookies for 10–15 minutes until golden brown, turning the trays halfway through baking. The lower trays will require a little more time than the upper ones.

Remove the trays from the oven. Leave the cookies on the trays for 5 minutes, so that they set, then transfer to a cooling rack using a spatula.

These cookies will keep for about 5 days stored in an airtight container.

Extremely chocolatey chocolate brownies
makes 24

I love chocolate brownies. In fact, I don't know anyone who doesn't love a chocolate brownie! These are very chocolatey indeed and contain cappuccino chocolate chips, which are available in good supermarkets. If you cannot find cappuccino chips, simply replace them with plain chocolate chunks and add a small shot of espresso to the brownie mixture for an added caffeine kick!

PREPARATION: 20 MINUTES | BAKING: 30–40 MINUTES

250g salted butter
350g plain chocolate
5 eggs
200g caster sugar
200g dark muscovado sugar
1 teaspoon vanilla extract
200g plain flour, sifted
200g cappuccino chocolate chips or plain
   chocolate chunks

equipment
large baking tin, 38 x 28cm, greased and lined
   (see page 8); heatproof bowl

Put the butter and plain chocolate in a heatproof bowl and leave this on top of the Aga until both have melted, stirring to remove any lumps. If you are short of time you can do this in a microwave by heating the bowl on full power for 40 seconds, stirring and then heating for a further 20–30 seconds or so until both the butter and chocolate have melted. Leave the mixture to cool.

In a bowl, whisk together the eggs, caster sugar and muscovado sugar, and vanilla until the mixture is thick and creamy and a pale yellow colour. Pour in the melted chocolate mixture, add the flour and cappuccino chips, and fold in gently using a spatula.

Pour the mixture into the baking tin and bake on the bottom shelf of the Roasting Oven under a cold shelf (or in the Baking Oven) for 30–40 minutes until a crust has formed on top of the cake but it still feels a little soft underneath. Turn the tray halfway through baking to ensure even cooking. Leave the cake to cool in the tray and then cut into slices to serve.

The brownies will keep in an airtight container for up to 3 days.

Chocolate chilli brownies
makes 15

Chocolate and chilli are one of those combinations that you wouldn't expect to work but nevertheless do. The chilli gives the cocoa a real depth of flavour and warmth. For a gentle chilli heat you can simply use ready-made chilli chocolate, which is available in most supermarkets, but for a more powerful chilli kick you can add some extra chilli powder if you wish. Half a teaspoon is definitely the most you will ever need; otherwise the brownies are too fiery! The chilli flavour is repeated in the icing and in the candied chilli decorations. (If you are not brave enough for the candied chillies, you can decorate the brownies with little red sugar hearts instead.)

PREPARATION: 20 MINUTES | BAKING: 30–40 MINUTES

for the brownies
200g plain chilli chocolate
150g plain chocolate
250g salted butter
5 eggs
200g caster sugar
200g light brown sugar
1/4–1/2 teaspoon chilli powder (optional)
200g plain flour

for the topping
100g chilli chocolate
150g plain chocolate

for the decoration
15 small chillies
200g caster sugar
200ml water

equipment
baking tin 38 x 28cm, greased and lined (see page 8); heatproof bowl; biscuit cutter, 7.5cm in diameter

Begin by making the chilli decorations. Simmer the sugar and water in a saucepan until you have a thin syrup. Add the chillies to the pan and simmer for about 10 minutes until they are soft. Remove from the heat and leave to cool in the syrup. (They can be made a day ahead of time and stored in an airtight jar until needed.)

Now make the brownies. Place the chilli chocolate, plain chocolate and butter in a heatproof bowl and place on top of the Aga (see page 9) until these ingredients have melted, stirring occasionally. If you are short of time you can do this in a microwave by heating the bowl on full power for 40 seconds, stirring and then heating for a further 20 or 30 seconds or so until both the butter and chocolate have melted. Leave the mixture to cool.

In a bowl, whisk together the eggs, caster sugar and light brown sugar until the mixture is thick and creamy and a pale yellow colour. Pour in the chocolate mixture, add the chilli powder (if using) and the flour, and fold in gently using a spatula.

Pour the mixture into the baking tin and bake on the bottom shelf of the Roasting Oven under a cold shelf (or in the Baking Oven) for 30–40 minutes until a crust has formed on top of the brownie but it still feels soft underneath. Turn the tray halfway through baking to ensure even cooking.

Leave the brownie to cool in the tray while you make the topping. Break both kinds of chocolate into pieces, place in a heatproof bowl and leave on top of the Aga until melted.

Using the biscuit cutter, cut 15 circles of the brownie and place them on a plate or tray. (The offcuts can be crumbled and sprinkled on to ice cream or simply discarded.)

Spread the melted chocolate over each of the brownies using a palette knife and top with a red chilli.

The brownies will keep in an airtight container for up to 3 days.

Coconut blondies
makes 24

These blondies (the white chocolate version of a brownie) are bursting with coconut and sweet cherries. Rich and fruity, they are perfect with a cup of tea. If you don't have any long shredded coconut, you can substitute desiccated coconut instead, but long shredded coconut is definitely worth finding as it is delicious and gives these blondies a chewy texture.

PREPARATION: 20 MINUTES | BAKING: 30–40 MINUTES

250g salted butter
350g white chocolate
160ml coconut cream
5 eggs
400g caster sugar
1 teaspoon vanilla extract
150g long shredded sweetened coconut (such as Baker's Angel Flake)
200g plain flour
200g glacé cherries, preferably the natural (dark) coloured, halved

equipment
heatproof bowl; baking tin, 38 x 28cm, greased and lined (see page 8) or a Baker's Edge Brownie Pan (as shown in the picture)

Place the butter, white chocolate and coconut cream in a heatproof bowl and leave on top of the Aga until melted, stirring occasionally. Leave the mixture to cool. I do not recommend melting white chocolate in a microwave as it can easily burn; but if you are short of time you can speed up the process by putting the bowl over a pan of simmering water on the Boiling Plate until the butter and chocolate are melted.

In a bowl, whisk together the eggs, caster sugar and vanilla until the mixture is thick and creamy and a pale yellow colour. Pour in the chocolate mixture, add the coconut and the flour, and fold in gently using a spatula. Stir in the cherries.

Pour the mixture into the prepared tin and bake on the bottom runners of the Roasting Oven under a cold shelf (or in the Baking Oven) for 30–40 minutes until a crust has formed on top of the blondie but it still feels soft underneath. Turn the tray halfway through baking to ensure even cooking. Leave the blondie to cool in the tray, then cut it into slices.

The blondies will keep for up to 3 days in an airtight container.

Sweet Things From the Aga

Apple crumble shortcake

makes 10 slices

This delicious, buttery crumble slice was inspired by the cakes I have eaten on trips to Germany; Streuselkuchen is one of my favourites. With soft poached apple and a buttery shortbread base, this traybake is great to serve for morning coffee or afternoon tea.

PREPARATION: 30 MINUTES | CHILLING: 30 MINUTES | BAKING: 20–30 MINUTES

for the shortcake

250g plain flour
120g caster sugar
1/2 teaspoon salt
225g butter, chilled and cut into cubes

for the apple layer

6 eating apples, peeled and cored
3 tablespoons caster sugar
juice of 1 lemon

for the crumble topping

150g self-raising flour
100g brown sugar
160g butter

equipment

baking tin 30 x 20cm, greased and lined (see page 8); potato masher

For the base, sift the plain flour into a bowl and stir in the sugar and salt. Rub the butter into the flour with your fingertips. Press into the base of the tin and then chill in the refrigerator for 30 minutes.

Cut the apples into small pieces. Place them in a saucepan with the caster sugar, lemon juice and 120ml water and cook on the Boiling Plate until the apple is soft, adding a little more water if necessary. Crush the apples lightly with a potato masher.

Bake the shortbread in the Roasting Oven below a cold shelf (or in the Baking Oven) for 10–15 minutes until light golden brown but still just soft. Remove the shortbread from the oven and leave to cool. Then spread the apple over the base.

For the topping, sift the flour and mix in the brown sugar, ensuring that any lumps are broken down. Cut the butter into cubes and rub it into the flour with your fingertips until it turns into uniform crumbs that are just coming together in small lumps.

Sprinkle the crumble over the apple and bake for a further 10–15 minutes in the bottom of the Roasting Oven below a cold shelf (or in the Baking Oven) until golden brown.

Leave the shortcake to cool in the tin and then cut into rectangles to serve.

The shortcake will keep for up to 3 days stored in an airtight container.

Maids of honour slices
makes 10 slices

The original maids of honour tart is said to have been created in Tudor times for Anne Boleyn and her attendants. Traditionally it consists of a buttery pastry case filled with jam and almond paste, similar to a bakewell tart. My version is made with croissant crumbs rather than breadcrumbs, for extra buttery flavour, and is baked in one large tart, to be cut into slices.

PREPARATION: 30 MINUTES | CHILLING: 1 HOUR | BAKING: 20–30 MINUTES

for the pastry
280g plain flour, sifted
1/2 teaspoon salt
140g butter, chilled and cut into cubes

for the filling
2 all-butter croissants
120g butter, softened
60g caster sugar
2 large eggs
1 teaspoon vanilla extract
150g ground almonds
zest of 1 lemon
5 tablespoons raspberry jam

to decorate
about 50 whole blanched almond halves
    (preferably Marcona)
icing sugar for dusting

equipment
30 x 20cm loose-bottomed cake tin, greased;
    blender or food processor

For the pastry, put the flour and salt in a mixing bowl. Rub the butter into the flour until it resembles fine breadcrumbs. Add about 2 tablespoons of cold water and mix in using a palette knife until the pastry comes together (add a little more water if needed). Wrap in cling film and chill in the refrigerator for 30 minutes.

On a flour-dusted surface, roll out the pastry thinly into a rectangle slightly larger than the size of the tin. Lift the pastry into the tin, using the rolling pin, and press into the tin with your fingers. Trim the edges of the pastry, prick the base with a fork and then transfer to the refrigerator to chill for 30 minutes.

In a blender or food processor, blitz the croissants to fine crumbs. Cream together the butter and sugar, then add the eggs, vanilla, ground almonds, lemon zest and croissant crumbs and mix everything well.

Remove the case from the refrigerator and spread the jam in a thin layer over the base. Cover the jam with the almond topping. Decorate with almonds and then bake in the Roasting Oven below a cold shelf (or in the Baking Oven) for about 20–30 minutes, turning the tin halfway through cooking.

Cut the tart into slices, dust with icing sugar and serve either warm or cold.

These slices will keep, stored in an airtight container, for up to 3 days.

Honey and sultana flapjacks
makes 12 slices

Flapjacks are very simple to prepare, and being packed full of oats and honey they give a real energy boost. They are the perfect treat for lunchboxes and picnics, as they travel well.

PREPARATION: 10 MINUTES | BAKING: 15–25 MINUTES

250g butter
200g caster sugar
4 tablespoons golden syrup
2 tablespoons clear (runny) honey
100g sultanas
400g porridge oats

equipment
baking tin 30 x 20cm, greased

Heat the butter, sugar, syrup and honey in a saucepan until the butter and sugar have melted.

Mix the sultanas and oats together in a bowl. Pour in the syrup mixture and stir well so that all the oats and fruit are coated in the syrup.

Spoon the mixture into the prepared tin and level the top with a spatula. Bake in the Roasting Oven below a cold shelf (or in the Baking Oven) for 15–25 minutes until golden brown, turning the tray halfway through cooking. Score into slices immediately, using a sharp knife, and then leave to cool in the tin.

The flapjacks will keep for up to 5 days in an airtight container.

Flapjack gingerbread

makes 15 squares

If you love gingerbread and flapjacks, then this is the traybake for you. A rich, treacly ginger cake topped with a syrup-coated oat layer – this is the perfect fireside treat on a cold afternoon with mugs of hot cocoa (for total self-indulgence, float marshmallows in the cocoa!).

PREPARATION: 30 MINUTES | BAKING: 35–45 MINUTES

for the gingerbread

115g butter
6 tablespoons black treacle
4 tablespoons golden syrup
115g dark muscovado sugar
140ml milk
2 eggs
225g plain flour
1 teaspoon bicarbonate of soda
2 teaspoons ground ginger

for the flapjack topping

125g butter
100g caster sugar
2 tablespoons golden syrup
200g porridge oats

equipment

deep roasting pan 30 x 20cm, greased and lined
  (see page 8)

Begin by preparing the gingerbread. Heat the butter, treacle, golden syrup and sugar in a saucepan until the butter has melted and the sugar has dissolved. Add the milk and leave to cool slightly. Beat in the eggs, whisking quickly after each.

Sift the flour, bicarbonate of soda and ginger into a mixing bowl. Pour in the treacle mixture and stir with a wooden spoon until everything is incorporated and there are no lumps of flour.

Pour the mixture into the roasting pan and bake in the Roasting Oven below a cold shelf (or in the Baking Oven) for 25–30 minutes until the cake is just firm but not cooked through (a cocktail stick inserted into the cake should emerge with some mixture sticking to it).

While the cake is baking, prepare the flapjack topping. Melt the butter, sugar and syrup in a saucepan, then stir in the oats, tossing well so that all the oats are coated with the syrup. Once the gingerbread has cooked for 25–30 minutes, remove the pan from the oven and carefully sprinkle the flapjack topping on top and spread it out evenly. Bake for a further 10–15 minutes in the Roasting Oven under a cold shelf (or the Baking Oven) until the topping is golden brown.

Remove the pan from the oven, leave the cake for 5 minutes and then cut it into 15 squares and leave to cool in the pan. You need to cut while the flapjack topping is still warm, as it is difficult to cut once set. Trim away any edges that have become too dark during baking.

This cake will keep for 3 days stored in an airtight container.

Sweet Things From the Aga

Orange Jaffa traybake
makes 16 slices

This zesty sponge traybake, inspired by the popular Jaffa cake, is flavoured with
orange curd and lemon zest and is the perfect tangy treat. Decorated with chocolate beans,
it makes a great cake for children's parties.

PREPARATION: 15 MINUTES | BAKING: 15–20 MINUTES

115g butter, softened
115g caster sugar
2 eggs
115g self-raising flour
50g Greek yoghurt
1 tablespoon orange curd
zest and juice of 1 lemon
zest and juice of 1 orange
2 heaped tablespoons icing sugar

to decorate
50g plain chocolate, melted
chocolate beans

equipment
2 disposable baking trays, 18 x 11cm

For the cake, whisk together the butter and
sugar until light and creamy. Beat in the eggs,
one at a time. Sift the flour and fold in, together
with the yoghurt, orange curd, and lemon and
orange zest.

Spoon the mixture into the trays and spread out
evenly. Bake in the Roasting Oven below a cold
shelf (or in the Baking Oven) for 15–20 minutes
until the cakes are golden brown and spring
back to your touch.

While the cakes are still warm, heat the orange
and lemon juice and the icing sugar in a
saucepan on the Boiling Plate until the sugar has
dissolved. Spoon this over the cake and leave to
cool.

Drizzle the cake with melted chocolate in thin
lines using a fork and sprinkle over the chocolate
beans. Cut into slices to serve.

This cake will store in an airtight container for
up to 2 days.

Plum frangipane slice
makes 24 slices

This light cinnamon sponge topped with juicy plums and pistachio frangipane – a variation on the traditional ground almonds – is delicious served either warm or cold. For an extra treat serve it with a dollop of clotted cream.

PREPARATION: 30 MINUTES | BAKING: 25–30 MINUTES

for the cake

225g butter
225g light muscovado sugar
4 eggs
225g self-raising flour
2 teaspoons ground cinnamon
2 tablespoons natural yoghurt

for the topping

500g plums
100g pistachios
125g butter
125g caster sugar
70g self-raising flour
icing sugar for dusting

equipment

large roasting pan 38 x 28cm, greased and lined (see page 8); food processor or blender

For the cake, cream together the butter and sugar until light and creamy. Beat in the eggs, one at a time. Sift in the flour and cinnamon and fold in, together with the yoghurt. Spoon the mixture into the roasting pan and spread out evenly.

Slice the plums in half and remove the stones. Place the plums, cut side down, on top of the cake.

For the frangipane topping, blitz the pistachios in a food processor until finely chopped. Place the pistachios, butter, sugar and flour in a mixing bowl and whisk together until creamy.

Place small spoonfuls of the pistachio mixture on top of the cake and spread out using a spatula or round-bladed knife. Bake in the Roasting Oven below a cold shelf (or in the Baking Oven) for 25–30 minutes until the cake is cooked through and a skewer comes out clean when inserted into the centre. Turn the cake halfway through baking.

Leave the cake to cool in the tin. Cut it into slices, then dust with icing sugar to serve.

The slices will store in an airtight container for up to 3 days.

Sweet Things From the Aga

Gluten-free almond scones
makes 10

These scones are made with ground almonds and gluten-free flour and are topped with an amaretto almond topping. Gluten-free flour can have a distinctive flavour, but the strong almond and lemon flavours included in the recipe mask this well.

PREPARATION: 20 MINUTES | BAKING: 10–20 MINUTES

200g gluten-free self-raising flour, sifted, plus extra for dusting
200g ground almonds
$1/4$ teaspoon salt
2 teaspoons baking powder
115g salted butter, chilled and cut into cubes, plus extra for greasing
60g caster sugar, plus extra for sprinkling
zest of 1 lemon
1 teaspoon vanilla extract
2 tablespoons amaretto liqueur
1 egg
100ml buttermilk
250ml milk, plus extra for brushing

for the topping
60g caster sugar
60g salted butter, softened
30g flaked almonds, plus extra for sprinkling
1 tablespoon gluten-free self-raising flour

equipment
baking tray lined with greaseproof paper or silicone mat; 8cm round, fluted biscuit cutter

Place the flour, ground almonds, salt and baking powder in a large mixing bowl. Rub the butter into the flour lightly with your fingertips until the mixture resembles fine breadcrumbs. Add the caster sugar, lemon zest, vanilla, amaretto, egg, buttermilk and milk, and mix to form a soft dough. The dough will seem very sticky at first, but the gluten-free flour will absorb the moisture as you mix.

On a lightly floured surface, gently roll out the scone dough to 2.5cm thickness using a flour-dusted rolling pin. Cut out the scones with the biscuit cutter, dusting it lightly in flour as you cut each scone to ensure a clean cut; this helps the scones to rise. Place the scones on the baking tray so that they are almost touching.

For the topping, mix together the sugar, butter, almonds and flour with a whisk and place a small mound of the mixture on top of each scone. Sprinkle a few flaked almonds on top.

Bake the scones in the middle of the Roasting Oven for 10–20 minutes until they are golden brown and sound hollow when you tap them. Turn the tray halfway through baking; cover it with a cold shelf if the scones start to brown too quickly. (Or use the Baking Oven, if available.)

Leave the scones on the baking tray for 5 minutes, then transfer them to a rack to cool.

These scones are best eaten on the day they are made but can be frozen and reheated.

Vanilla scones
makes 10

Scones are one of those quick and easy recipes that are so very popular. Made with everyday store-cupboard ingredients, they are a great standby and are delicious served with clotted cream and strawberries.

PREPARATION: 15 MINUTES | BAKING: 10–20 MINUTES

450g self-raising flour, sifted, plus extra for dusting
1/4 teaspoon salt
1 teaspoon baking powder
125g salted butter, chilled and cut into cubes, plus extra for greasing
60g vanilla sugar, plus extra for sprinkling
250ml milk, plus extra for brushing
1 teaspoon vanilla extract

equipment
baking tray lined with greaseproof paper or silicone mat; 8cm round, fluted biscuit cutter

Place the flour, salt and baking powder in a large mixing bowl. Rub the cubes of butter into the flour lightly with your fingertips until the mixture resembles fine breadcrumbs. Add the vanilla sugar and milk and mix to form a soft dough. Add a little more milk if the mixture is too dry.

On a lightly floured surface, gently roll out the dough to 2.5cm thickness using a flour-dusted rolling pin. Cut out the scones with the biscuit cutter, dusting the cutter lightly in flour as you cut each scone to ensure a clean cut; this helps the scones to rise.

Place the scones on the baking tray so that they are almost touching. Mix a few tablespoons of extra milk with the vanilla extract and brush this over the tops of the scones using a pastry brush. Sprinkle a little sugar on top.

Bake the scones in the middle of the Roasting Oven for 10–20 minutes until they are golden brown and sound hollow when you tap them. Turn the tray halfway through cooking; cover it with a cold shelf if the scones start to brown too quickly. (Or use the Baking Oven, if available.)

After removing the scones from the oven, leave them on the baking tray for 5 minutes, then transfer to a rack to cool.

These scones are best eaten on the day they are made but can be frozen and reheated.

Sweet Things From the Aga

Homemade clotted cream

Although clotted cream is readily available in supermarkets, it is very easy to make your own with an Aga. This clotted cream has a delicious caramel flavour as a result of being baked and is perfect to serve with scones and jam.

PREPARATION: 5 MINUTES
COOKING: ABOUT 3 HOURS

300ml double cream

Pour the cream into a 24 x 16cm Aga-proof dish and place it in the Simmering Oven. Leave it for about 3 hours, until a golden skin has formed on top of the cream and it feels set below, although still with a slight wobble. Leave to cool before serving.

Blueberry scones
makes 10

These feather-light scones are bursting with blueberries and are delicious served warm,
spread with lashings of butter. For an extra-special treat, serve them with blueberry jam as well.

PREPARATION: 15 MINUTES | BAKING: 10–20 MINUTES

450g self-raising flour, sifted, plus extra for
   dusting
$1/_4$ teaspoon salt
1 teaspoon baking powder
125g salted butter, chilled and cut into cubes,
   plus extra for greasing
60g caster sugar, plus extra for sprinkling
1 teaspoon vanilla extract
250ml milk, plus extra for brushing
150g blueberries

equipment
baking tray lined with greaseproof paper or
   silicone mat; 8cm round, fluted biscuit cutter

Place the flour, salt and baking powder in a large mixing bowl. Rub the butter into the flour lightly with your fingertips until the mixture resembles fine breadcrumbs. Add the caster sugar, vanilla and milk, and mix to form a soft dough. Add a little more milk if the mixture is too dry. Add the blueberries to the bowl and gently fold into the dough.

On a lightly floured surface, gently roll out the scone dough to 2.5cm thickness using a flour-dusted rolling pin. Cut out the scones with the biscuit cutter, dusting it lightly in flour as you cut each scone to ensure a clean cut; this helps the scones to rise.

Place the scones on the baking tray so that they are almost touching. Brush the tops with milk, using a pastry brush, and sprinkle with a little caster sugar.

Bake the scones in the middle of the Roasting Oven for 10–20 minutes until they are golden brown and sound hollow when you tap them. Turn the tray halfway through baking; cover it with a cold shelf if the scones start to brown too quickly. (Or use the Baking Oven, if available.)

Leave the scones on the baking tray for 5 minutes, then transfer them to a rack to cool.

These scones are best eaten on the day they are made but can be frozen and reheated.

Wholemeal apple and cranberry scones

makes 8

These wholesome scones are bursting with apple and cranberries and make a healthy afternoon treat, served with a low-fat spread. For a little self-indulgence, serve them with apple butter (see recipe below) and whipped cream.

PREPARATION: 15 MINUTES | BAKING: 10–20 MINUTES

200g self-raising flour, plus extra for dusting
250g wholemeal self-raising flour
1 teaspoon baking powder
125g salted butter, chilled and cut into cubes, plus extra for greasing
60g light muscovado sugar
1 teaspoon ground cinnamon
2 dessert apples, cored and grated
1 teaspoon vanilla extract
100g dried cranberries
200ml milk, plus extra for brushing
caster sugar for dusting

for the apple butter
5 eating apples (such as Granny Smiths)
1 lemon
80g caster sugar
1 tablespoon butter

to serve
whipped cream

equipment
baking tray lined with greaseproof paper or silicone mat

Sift the flours and baking powder into a large mixing bowl. Rub the chilled butter lightly into the flour with your fingertips until the mixture resembles fine breadcrumbs. Add the sugar, cinnamon, grated apples, vanilla and cranberries, and stir. Add the milk gradually, mixing to form a soft dough. Add a little more milk if the mixture is too dry.

On a lightly floured surface, gently roll out the dough into a circle approximately 20–25cm in diameter. Using a sharp knife, score the dough into 8 segments. Place the round on the baking tray and brush with milk and sprinkle with caster sugar.

Bake the scone in the middle of the Roasting Oven for 10–20 minutes until golden brown and the scone sounds hollow when you tap it. Turn the tray halfway through cooking; cover the scone with a cold shelf if it starts to brown too quickly. (Or use the Baking Oven, if available.)

For the apple butter, peel and core the apples and cut into small pieces. Place in a saucepan with the juice of the lemon and 200ml water, and simmer until the apple is soft and mushy, adding a little more water if it evaporates. Add the sugar and cook until the sugar has dissolved. Add the butter and stir until melted. Remove from the heat and set aside to cool.

Serve the scones warm with the apple butter and whipped cream.

These scones are best eaten on the day they are made but can be frozen and reheated.

Sweet Things From the Aga

Rose and saffron scones
makes 10

Flavoured with hints of the Far East – with saffron and rose syrup – and topped with pretty rose petals, these are the perfect scones for high tea. Always use pesticide-free roses – those that have not been sprayed with any chemicals during growing.

PREPARATION: 15 MINUTES | BAKING: 10–20 MINUTES

250ml milk, plus extra for brushing
$^1/_2$ teaspoon (a generous pinch) saffron threads
450g self-raising flour, sifted, plus extra for dusting
$^1/_4$ teaspoon salt
1 teaspoon baking powder
125g salted butter, chilled and cut into cubes, plus extra for greasing
60g caster sugar, plus extra for sprinkling
1 tablespoon rose syrup

to glaze
30ml rose syrup
2 tablespoons caster sugar

to decorate
3 tablespoons shredded fresh rose petals (pesticide free)

equipment
baking tray lined with greaseproof paper or silicone mat; 8cm round, fluted biscuit cutter

Heat the milk and saffron and then leave to infuse until the milk cools, by which time the milk will have taken on a golden yellow colour.

Place the flour, salt and baking powder in a large mixing bowl. Rub the chilled butter into the flour lightly with your fingertips until the mixture resembles fine breadcrumbs. Add the caster sugar, rose syrup and saffron-infused milk and mix to form a soft dough. Add a little more milk if the mixture is too dry.

On a lightly floured surface, gently roll out the dough to 2.5cm thickness using a flour-dusted rolling pin. Cut out the scones with the cutter, dusting it lightly in flour as you cut each scone to ensure a clean cut; this helps the scones to rise. Place the scones on the baking tray so that they are almost touching. Mix the rose syrup with a little milk and brush the tops of the scones with this, using a pastry brush; sprinkle a little caster sugar on top.

Bake in the middle of the Roasting Oven for 10–20 minutes until the scones are golden brown and sound hollow when you tap them. Turn the tray halfway through cooking; cover with a cold shelf if the scones start to brown too quickly. (Or use the Baking Oven, if available.)

Leave the scones on the baking tray for 5 minutes, then transfer to a rack to cool. For the glaze, heat the rose syrup with the caster sugar until the sugar dissolves. Leave to cool. Brush the syrup over the tops of the scones and sprinkle the shredded rose petals on top. Serve straight away.

These scones are best eaten on the day they are made, but can be frozen (albeit without the rose petal topping) and reheated to serve.

Toffee hazelnut scones
makes 12

These nutty scones are topped with a buttery caramel sauce and are delectable simply served warm with butter.

PREPARATION: 15 MINUTES | BAKING: 10–20 MINUTES

450g self-raising flour, sifted, plus extra for dusting
1/4 teaspoon salt
1 teaspoon baking powder
125g salted butter, chilled and cut into cubes, plus extra for greasing
1 tablespoon caster sugar, plus extra for sprinkling
2 tablespoons of the toffee sauce (recipe below)
75g chopped roasted hazelnuts
250ml milk, plus extra for brushing

for the toffee sauce

30g caster sugar
30g soft dark brown sugar
30g butter
90ml double cream
1 tablespoon golden syrup

equipment

baking tray lined with greaseproof paper or silicone mat; 8cm triangle cutter

Begin by making the toffee sauce, as you need to add some of this to the scone mixture. Simmer all the toffee sauce ingredients together in a saucepan on the Simmering Plate until the sugar has dissolved and then set aside to cool.

Place the flour, salt and baking powder in a large mixing bowl. Rub the chilled butter into the flour lightly with your fingertips until the mixture resembles fine breadcrumbs. Stir in the caster sugar, 2 tablespoons of toffee sauce and two-thirds of the hazelnuts. Add the milk gradually and mix to form a soft dough. You may not need all of the milk.

On a lightly floured surface, gently roll out the dough to 2.5cm thickness using a flour-dusted rolling pin. Cut out the scones with the biscuit cutter, dusting it lightly in flour as you cut each scone to ensure a clean cut; this helps the scones to rise.

Place the scones on the baking tray so that they are a small distance apart. Brush the top of the scones with milk, using a pastry brush, and sprinkle with caster sugar and the remaining nuts. Bake in middle of the Roasting Oven for 10–20 minutes until the scones are golden brown and sound hollow when you tap them. Turn the tray halfway through to ensure even cooking; cover with a cold shelf if the scones start to brown too much. (Or use the Baking Oven, if available.)

Leave the scones on the baking tray for 5 minutes, then transfer to a rack to cool. Brush the tops of the scones generously with the remaining toffee sauce and serve warm with butter.

These scones are best eaten on the day they are made.

Sweet Things From the Aga

Fancy Things

Cardamom and pistachio macarons
makes 16

These delicate macarons, inspired by the great French patisseries of Pierre Hermé and Ladurée, are scented with one of my favourite spices, cardamom. Its tiny black seeds produce a heady and exotic scent and are a perfect complement to the pistachios. Dusted with gold lustre powder, these macarons are the ultimate luxury baking.

PREPARATION: 25 MINUTES | BAKING: 25–30 MINUTES

for the macarons
8 green cardamom pods
85g caster sugar
100g pistachios, plus extra, chopped, for sprinkling
20g ground almonds
175g icing sugar
3 egg whites
gold edible lustre powder
edible glitter (optional)

for the cream
250ml double cream
1 tablespoon rose syrup
1 tablespoon icing sugar

equipment
pestle and mortar; food processor; 2 Aga cold shelves lined with silicone mats; 2 piping bags, 1 fitted with a large round nozzle and 1 with a large star nozzle

Remove the black seeds from the cardamom pods and grind in the mortar, along with a teaspoon of the caster sugar, until you have a fine powder.

Place the pistachios, ground almonds and icing sugar in the food processor and blitz to a fine powder. Sieve the nut powder into a bowl; return any pieces that do not pass through the sieve to the blender, blitz, then sieve again.

Whisk the egg whites to stiff peaks and then add the remaining caster sugar, a spoonful at a time, until the meringue is smooth and glossy. Add the nut powder, a third at a time, folding in with a spatula together with the ground cardamom. The important thing is to get the meringue to the right texture. It needs to be folded until it is just soft enough that it will not quite hold a peak.

Drop a little of the mixture onto a plate; if it settles into a smooth surface, it is ready. If it holds a peak then you need to fold it a few more times. If you fold it too much it will be too runny and the macarons will not hold their shape.

Spoon the mixture into a piping bag with the round nozzle and pipe 32 rounds, 4cm in diameter, on to the baking trays, placing them a small distance apart, as they will spread during cooking. Sprinkle a few chopped pistachios on to half of the rounds (the macaron tops), if you wish. Leave the macarons on the trays for 30 minutes so that a skin forms on them; this will give them their classic sugar-crusted edge.

Bake the macarons in the middle of the Simmering Oven for 5 minutes, then transfer to the bottom runners of the Roasting Oven and cook for 5 minutes (turn the trays halfway through so that they are evenly cooked, covering with the cold shelf if they start to brown too much), then return to the Simmering Oven and cook for a further 15–20 minutes until the macarons are set. Remove from the oven and leave to cool on the trays.

For the filling, whisk the double cream, rose syrup and icing sugar to stiff peaks, spoon into the piping bag fitted with the star nozzle and pipe stars of cream onto the flat side of half of the macaron shells. Top each with a pistachio-topped macaron shell. Dust the tops of the macarons with gold lustre powder and sprinkle with edible glitter if you wish.

Because the macarons contain fresh cream they should be stored in the refrigerator and eaten within 2 days.

Peanut meringues
makes 18

Among the easiest things to bake in the Aga are meringues: the Simmering Oven is the perfect temperature for achieving a crisp shell with a gooey centre. For this recipe the meringues are filled with a peanut cream, but you can vary the flavour, adding a little melted chocolate for a chocolate cream, a tablespoon of rose syrup for rose cream or a few drops of peppermint essence for peppermint cream, if you prefer. The meringues can also be decorated in a variety of ways. Why not try sprinkling chopped pistachios or flaked almonds on top before baking? Sugar sprinkles also work well and look very pretty.

PREPARATION: 15 MINUTES | BAKING: 1–1¹/₄ HOURS

for the meringues
3 egg whites
170g caster sugar
3 tablespoons honey-roasted peanuts, finely chopped

for the filling
200ml double cream
1 heaped tablespoon smooth peanut butter

equipment
2 cold shelves or large baking trays lined with silicone mats or baking parchment, 2 piping bags fitted with a large star nozzle; 18 cake cases for serving

For the meringue, whisk the egg whites to stiff peaks in a large bowl. While still whisking, add the caster sugar, one tablespoonful at a time, until all the sugar is incorporated. The meringue should be glossy and hold a peak when you lift the beaters.

Spoon the meringue into one of the piping bags and pipe 36 stars of meringue, 4cm in diameter, on to the silicone mats. Place them a distance apart, as they will spread during cooking (and take care not to position them at the edges of the tray, otherwise they might touch the sides of the Aga). Sprinkle the chopped peanuts on top of the meringues. Slide the trays on to the middle and bottom runners of the Simmering Oven and bake for 1–1¹/₄ hours until the meringues are crisp and slightly golden (the bottom tray will take slightly longer to cook). Leave the meringues to cool.

Place the double cream and peanut butter in a mixing bowl and whip with an electric or hand whisk to stiff peaks. Spoon the cream into the second piping bag and sandwich pairs of the meringues together with a star of cream. Place in cake cases to serve.

Because the meringues contain fresh cream they should be stored in the refrigerator until you are ready to serve; however, the meringue shells will keep for a week in a sealed container before being filled with the cream. Once filled, they are best eaten the same day, although they will keep until the next day stored in the refrigerator.

Treacle loaf cakes with lemon icing
makes 12

Rich, dark treacle and tangy lemon are the perfect pairing in these little teatime cakes. If you prefer, you can replace the cream cheese icing with a simple lemon icing by mixing icing sugar with a little lemon juice and then drizzling this over the cakes.

PREPARATION: 30 MINUTES | BAKING: 20–25 MINUTES

115g butter, softened
100g caster sugar
1 tablespoon black treacle
2 eggs
115g self-raising flour
1 teaspoon ground cinnamon
1 teaspoon ground ginger
zest of 1 lemon

for the icing

30g butter, softened
75g cream cheese
1 tablespoon lemon juice
150g icing sugar, sifted

to decorate

1 lemon
1 tablespoon caster sugar

equipment

12-hole mini loaf tin (each mini loaf 8 x 3cm), greased; piping bag fitted with a large star nozzle; zester

For the cakes, first cream together the butter, sugar and treacle until light and creamy.
Beat in the eggs, one at a time. Sift in the flour, cinnamon and ginger, add the lemon zest, and fold in.

Spoon the mixture into each hole of the mini-loaf tin and bake on the middle runners of the Roasting Oven below a cold shelf (or the Baking Oven) for 20–25 minutes until the cakes spring back to your touch, turning the tray halfway through to ensure even cooking.
Turn the cakes out on to a rack to cool.

For the icing, whisk together the butter, cream cheese, lemon juice and icing sugar until smooth. Spoon into the piping bag and pipe a swirl of icing on top of each cake.

To decorate, peel long strands of lemon zest, using a zester, and squeeze the juice from the lemon. Simmer the zest in the lemon juice and caster sugar for a few minutes in a saucepan placed on the Boiling Plate. Strain and leave to cool, then place a little lemon zest on top of each cake to serve.

The cakes are best eaten on the day they are made but will keep for up to 3 days in an airtight container.

Strawberry cream cupcakes
makes 10

At the height of summer, when strawberries are ripe and juicy, these little cakes make the perfect afternoon teatime treat. Filled with a delicious fresh strawberry cream and topped with a whole strawberry, they look almost (but not really!) too pretty to eat. If you do not have a cupcake plunger (a device that removes the core from a cupcake) you can cut away the centre using a sharp knife instead.

PREPARATION: 20 MINUTES | BAKING: 15–20 MINUTES

115g butter, softened
115g caster sugar
2 eggs
85g self-raising flour
60g ground almonds
1 teaspoon vanilla extract
1 heaped tablespoon ricotta cheese

for the strawberry filling
100g strawberries, hulled
1 heaped tablespoon icing sugar
250ml double cream

to assemble
10 small strawberries
icing sugar for dusting

equipment
muffin tin filled with 10 muffin cases; food processor; cupcake plunger (optional); piping bag fitted with a large star nozzle

For the cakes, cream together the butter and sugar until light and creamy. Beat in the eggs, one at a time. Sift in the flour and fold in the ground almonds, together with the vanilla and ricotta.

Spoon the mixture into the muffin cases and bake on the middle runners of the Roasting Oven below a cold shelf (or in the Baking Oven) for 15–20 minutes until the cakes are golden brown and spring back to your touch and when a clean skewer inserted into the centre of one of the muffins comes out clean. Turn the tray halfway through baking to ensure even cooking. Cool the cakes on a wire rack.

For the filling, blitz the strawberries and icing sugar together in a food processor to a smooth purée.

Whip the cream to stiff peaks, then fold half of the strawberry purée through the cream using a spatula. Spoon the cream into the piping bag.

Use the cupcake plunger to remove the centre of each cake. If you don't have a plunger, cut out a hollow using a knife. Place a spoonful of the remaining strawberry purée in each hole and then pipe a star of cream on top. Dust with icing sugar, drizzle over a little strawberry purée and top each cake with a strawberry.

Because these cakes contain fresh cream they should be served straight away or stored in the refrigerator until needed. They are best eaten on the day they are made.

Margarita loaf cakes
makes 8

Margaritas are one of my favourite cocktails – I love the tangy tequila, salt and the zing of lime. All these elements are wrapped up in these little cakes. If you don't like tequila, you can simply omit it from the recipe and make mini lime cakes instead.

PREPARATION: 20 MINUTES | BAKING: 15–20 MINUTES

115g butter, softened
115g caster sugar
2 eggs
115g self-raising flour
zest of 2 limes
80ml natural yoghurt

for the syrup
2 tablespoons tequila
juice of 3 limes
2 tablespoons icing sugar

for the icing
6 tablespoons fondant icing sugar
juice of 1 lime
a few drops of green food colouring
flaked sea salt for sprinkling
8 jelly lime slices

equipment
8 mini loaf baking cases, 10 x 5cm

For the cakes, whisk together the butter and sugar until light and creamy. Beat in the eggs, one at a time. Sift in the flour and fold in the lime zest and yoghurt.

Spoon the mixture into the loaf cases, place on a baking tray and bake on the middle runners of the Roasting Oven below a cold shelf (or in the Baking Oven) for 15–20 minutes until the cakes are golden brown and spring back to your touch and when a skewer inserted into the centre comes out clean. Turn the tray halfway through baking to ensure even cooking.

While the cakes are still warm, heat the tequila, lime juice and icing sugar in a saucepan on the Simmering Plate until the sugar has dissolved and then drizzle a little of this syrup over each cake.

For the icing, mix together the icing sugar, lime juice and a few drops of green food colouring plus a little water until you have a smooth icing. Spoon the icing onto each cake. Sprinkle a few flakes of sea salt on top and a jelly lime slice and leave for the icing to set.

These cakes will keep for up to 2 days in an airtight container.

Sweet Things From the Aga

Pumpkin muffins
makes 12

Pumpkin – essential to Halloween and American Thanksgiving celebrations – is delicious in these buttery spiced muffins. They are best served warm from the Aga. Tinned pumpkin purée is available from good supermarkets – I use Libby's pumpkin purée – but you can prepare your own at home by roasting pumpkin (or butternut squash) which has been peeled, deseeded and cut into small pieces. Wrap them in foil with a little water and maple syrup and place in the roasting oven until the flesh is soft. Finally, purée in a food processor until smooth.

PREPARATION: 15 MINUTES | BAKING: 15–20 MINUTES

100g butter
250g self-raising flour
1 teaspoon bicarbonate of soda
1 teaspoon baking powder
2 teaspoons vanilla extract
1 tablespoon ginger syrup
2 teaspoons ground cinnamon
100g caster sugar
100g pecan nuts, chopped
150ml milk
100g Greek yoghurt
2 eggs
100g pumpkin purée

equipment
12-hole muffin tin lined with 12 muffin cases

Place the butter in a heatproof bowl on top of the Aga to melt it, then leave to cool.
Sift the flour, bicarbonate of soda and baking powder into a bowl. Add the vanilla, ginger syrup, cinnamon, sugar and chopped pecans and mix well.

Whisk together the milk, yoghurt and eggs and mix into the flour mixture. Pour in the cooled butter, add the pumpkin purée, and whisk again. Spoon the mixture into the muffin cases.

Bake on the middle runners of the Roasting Oven below a cold shelf (or in the Baking Oven) for 15–20 minutes, turning the tray halfway through cooking. Leave the muffins to cool on a rack.

These muffins will keep for up to 2 days in an airtight container but are best eaten on the day they are made.

Blueberry and orange muffins
makes 12

Everyone loves that all-American favourite the blueberry muffin. This version, bursting with berries and with a tang of orange, makes a delicious treat at any time of day. Why not serve the muffins warm for breakfast, straight from the Aga with a fresh pot of coffee?

PREPARATION: 15 MINUTES | BAKING: 15–20 MINUTES

100g butter
250g self-raising flour
1 teaspoon bicarbonate of soda
1 teaspoon baking powder
100g dark brown sugar
150ml milk
125ml natural yoghurt
2 eggs
zest and juice of 1 orange
200g blueberries
1 tablespoon icing sugar

equipment
12-hole muffin tin lined with 12 muffin cases

Place the butter in a heatproof bowl on top of the Aga to melt it, then remove it from the Aga and leave it to cool.

Sift the flour, bicarbonate of soda and baking powder into a bowl and stir in the sugar. Whisk together the milk, yoghurt and eggs. Pour this into the flour mixture, add the cooled butter and whisk again. Fold in the orange zest and blueberries. (Don't worry if the batter is slightly lumpy; this is normal.)

Spoon the mixture into the muffin cases and bake for 15–20 minutes on the middle rungs of the Roasting Oven below a cold shelf (or in the Baking Oven), turning the tin halfway through cooking.

When the muffins are baked, heat the orange juice and icing sugar and bring to the boil on the Boiling Plate. Spoon a little of the syrup over each muffin. You may not need all of the syrup, depending on how juicy your orange was.

These muffins will keep for 2 days in an airtight container but are best on the day they are made.

Sweet Things From the Aga

Pecan madeleines
makes 16

These delicious light and airy cakes are quick and easy to prepare. They may look plain but they have a surprising depth of flavour and go perfectly with a cup of tea. You can make mini madeleines, if you prefer, in a mini madeleine tin, and just reduce the cooking time slightly. Chilling the batter is an important step so don't be tempted to skip it.

PREPARATION: 15 MINUTES | CHILLING: 1 HOUR |
BAKING: 10–15 MINUTES PER TRAY

50g pecans
2 eggs
80g caster sugar
90g self-raising flour, sifted
1 teaspoon ground cinnamon
1 tablespoon maple syrup
1 teaspoon vanilla extract
100g butter, melted and cooled
icing sugar for dusting

equipment
food processor; 2 madeleine pans, greased
   (or cook in batches if you have only one pan,
   washing the pan between uses); piping bag

Blitz the pecans very finely in a food processor.

In a separate bowl, whisk together the eggs and sugar until light and creamy. Add the flour, ground pecans, cinnamon, maple syrup and vanilla, and whisk again. Pour in the cooled melted butter, fold through using a spatula, and spoon into a piping bag. Chill the mixture in the fridge for 1 hour.

Pipe a little of the mixture into each of the madeleine moulds and bake for 10–15 minutes on the middle runners of the Roasting Oven below a cold shelf (or in the Baking Oven) until golden brown. If you have only one madeleine pan, bake in batches, storing the uncooked batter in the fridge while the first batch is cooking. Turn out on to a rack to cool.

Dust the madeleines with icing sugar to serve.

These are best eaten on the day they are made.

Spiced chocolate doughnuts
makes 14

Although doughnuts take a bit of effort and patience, homemade doughnuts are much nicer than shop-bought ones. These cinnamon doughnuts contain a spiced chocolate cream with a hint of orange. They were inspired by the amazing chef Simon Rogan, who served mini doughnuts with coffee when I ate at his restaurant, L'Enclume – they tasted of Christmas morning with chocolate and spices, and I have never forgotten them!

PREPARATION: 30 MINUTES | PROVING: 1 HOUR | COOKING: 10 MINUTES

200ml warm milk
7g fast-action dried yeast
30g caster sugar, plus extra for coating the
    doughnuts
300g plain flour, plus extra for dusting
160g strong flour
$1/2$ teaspoon salt
2 eggs
3 teaspoons ground cinnamon (separated: 2 and
    1 teaspoons)
zest of 1 orange
60g butter, softened
sunflower or vegetable oil for frying
    (approximately 1–2 litres, depending on size
    of fryer/pan)

for the filling
100g spiced plain chocolate (such as Green &
    Black's Maya Gold)
1 tablespoon butter
300ml double cream

equipment
deep-fat fryer (optional); sugar thermometer;
    piping bag with round nozzle; 14 squares of
    baking parchment, approximately 8x8cm; food
    processor; stand mixer with dough hook; trivet

Place the warm milk, yeast and caster sugar in a jug, whisk together and leave on top of the Aga to warm for about 10 minutes until a thick foam has formed on top of the milk.

Meanwhile, sift the plain and strong flours into a large mixing bowl, add the salt, eggs, 2 teaspoons of the ground cinnamon, orange zest and butter, and mix together to incorporate, then pour in the yeast mixture.

Using a stand mixer fitted with a dough hook, mix the dough on a slow speed for 2 minutes, then increase the speed and knead for about 8 minutes until the dough is very soft and pliable.

Lay the squares of baking parchment on a cold shelf and dust with flour. Divide the dough into 14 small balls and, first dusting your hands with flour, shape each into a ball and place one on each piece of baking parchment. Cover with a clean, damp tea towel and leave to rest for 10 minutes.

Reshape the balls, then prove them on a tray placed on the trivet on top of the Simmering Plate for about 35–45 minutes, covered in lightly greased cling film, until each doughnut has doubled in size and the dough just holds an indent when you press with your finger tips. Leave to rest, uncovered, for 10 minutes.

Pour the oil into a saucepan placed on the Boiling Plate or a deep-fat fryer, and heat to 190°C. When the oil has reached this temperature, tip each doughnut into the oil, carefully sliding it off the paper so that you do not touch the dough or the hot oil. Fry the doughnuts in batches of 3 or 4, cooking on each side for about $1^1/2$ minutes until golden brown.

Remove the doughnuts from the oil, using a slotted spoon, and drain on kitchen paper. Mix the remaining cinnamon with caster sugar and roll each doughnut in the sugar while still warm. Use a teaspoon handle to poke a hole in the doughnut and move it around to make a cavity inside. Leave to cool.

For the filling, melt the chocolate and butter in a bowl on top of the Aga. Leave to cool then add the cream and whip to stiff peaks. Spoon the filling into a piping bag fitted with a round nozzle and pipe the cream into each of the doughnuts.

These doughnuts should be eaten on the day they are made.

Fancy Things

Fig and mascarpone slices
makes 8 slices

These flaky pastry slices are ideal for picnics. Baked with mascarpone cheese and sprinkled with a light dusting of caramelised sugar, they are the perfect taste of summer.

PREPARATION: 20 MINUTES | BAKING: 10–20 MINUTES

500g puff pastry
250g mascarpone cheese
1 small egg
1 tablespoon caster sugar, plus extra for
   sprinkling
8 ripe figs
milk for glazing

equipment
cold shelf lined with baking parchment or
   silicone mat

Dust a clean work surface with flour and roll out the pastry to 5mm thickness. Cut out 8 rectangles of pastry, 10 x 6cm in size, using a sharp knife, and place on the baking tray. Score a line with a sharp knife around the edge of each pastry slice about 1cm from the edge, taking care not to cut all the way through.

Bake the slices on the middle shelf of the Roasting Oven for 5 minutes; turn the tray and bake for a further 3 minutes (cover with a cold shelf if they start to brown too much). Remove them from the oven and press down the central panel of pastry.

Whisk together the mascarpone, egg and caster sugar and divide between the pastry cases.

Cut each fig into thin slices and lay the slices in a fan pattern on top of the mascarpone. Brush the pastry with milk to glaze, using a pastry brush, and sprinkle each pastry slice with caster sugar.

Return the slices to the Roasting Oven and cook for a further 5–10 minutes until the sugar has caramelised. Cover the slices with a cold shelf if the pastry starts to brown too much. Remove from the oven and leave to cool before serving.

The slices can be stored in the refrigerator for up to 2 days.

Sweet Things From the Aga

Churros with salted caramel sauce
makes 30

Hot churros are a traditional Spanish snack, enjoyed also in Latin America and many other parts of the world. Made from a light choux batter which is deep-fried then usually coated in caster sugar, they are light and delicious. I like to serve my churros with a warm salted caramel dipping sauce for an extra-special treat!

PREPARATION: 20 MINUTES | COOKING: ABOUT 20 MINUTES

115g self-raising flour
100g butter
3 large eggs, beaten
sunflower oil for frying (approximately
    1–2 litres, depending on size of fryer)
caster sugar for sprinkling

for the sauce
100g caster sugar
pinch of salt
70g butter
120ml double cream

equipment
piping bag fitted with a large star nozzle or a
    cookie press; large saucepan; sugar
    thermometer

Sift the flour twice to remove all lumps and to add as much air as possible. Place 250ml water in a saucepan with the butter and simmer on the Simmering Plate until the butter has melted. Bring to the boil, then quickly tip in all the flour in one go and beat hard with a wooden spoon until a ball of dough forms. Leave to cool for 10 minutes then beat in the eggs, adding the egg mixture a little at a time and beating after each addition.

Spoon the mixture into a piping bag fitted with a star nozzle or the cookie press. Pour the sunflower oil into a large pan to a depth of about 8–10cm. (Make sure to use a pan with a level base so that it sits flat on the Boiling Plate to ensure even contact and cooking.) Heat the oil on the Boiling Plate to 190°C.

Pipe the mixture into the pan in lengths of about 10cm, holding the piping bag in one hand and a pair of kitchen scissors in the other. Use the scissors to cut the dough at the desired length. If you are using a cookie press, pipe in lengths of dough. Take care that the oil does not splash, as it can burn. Cook about 5 churros at a time and do not overfill the pan. Cook for about 3–5 minutes, then turn the churros on to the other side and cook until they are golden brown all over.

Place the cooked churros on sheets of kitchen paper to drain the oil, then transfer to a plate of caster sugar and dust well.

For the sauce, place the sugar, salt and butter in a saucepan and heat on the Boiling Plate, stirring all the time, until the butter melts and sugar dissolves. The mixture will start to turn a golden brown. Stir all the time so that the caramel doesn't burn.

Remove the pan from the heat and let the caramel cool for a few minutes. Add the cream to the pan, return to the Boiling Plate and stir until the toffee sauce is thick. Serve the churros soon after cooking, dipping them into the warm sauce.

Once cooked, the churros should be eaten straight away; however, you can freeze the uncooked piped churros and then deep-fry them from frozen.

Hazelnut praline éclairs
makes 12 éclairs

If you are a fan of Nutella, then these are the pastry treat for you – light choux pastry with chocolate hazelnut cream, topped with a chocolate fondant icing. Or, if you like Reese's peanut butter chocolates, simply replace the Nutella with peanut butter and sprinkle finely chopped peanuts on top as a delicious alternative.

PREPARATION: 25 MINUTES | BAKING: ABOUT 20 MINUTES

for the pastry
65g plain flour
50g butter
2 eggs

for the filling
1 heaped tablespoon Nutella
200ml double cream

to decorate
250g fondant icing sugar, sifted
2 tablespoons cocoa powder, sifted
2 tablespoons roasted and chopped hazelnuts

equipment
Baking trays, greased and lined; piping bag fitted
   with a medium round nozzle

Sieve the flour twice to remove any lumps. Heat the butter in a saucepan with 150ml water on the Boiling Plate until the butter is melted, bring to the boil, then quickly add the sifted flour all at once and remove from the heat. Beat hard with a wooden spoon or whisk until the dough forms a ball and no longer sticks to the sides of the pan. Leave to cool for about 5 minutes.

Whisk the eggs and then beat into the pastry, a little at a time, using a balloon whisk or a wooden spoon. The mixture will form a sticky paste which holds its shape when you lift the whisk up.

Spoon the pastry into the piping bag and pipe 12 lengths of pastry, about 6–8 cm in length, on to the baking sheets, a small distance apart. Wet your finger and smooth down any peaks left from the piping.

Bake the éclairs on the middle runners of the Roasting Oven for about 15 minutes until crisp; then, with a sharp knife, cut a small slit in each éclair and return to the oven for 5 minutes until crisp. If the pastry starts to brown too much, cover it with a cold shelf. Cool the éclairs on a rack and then cut each one in half.

Add the Nutella to the double cream and whip to stiff peaks. Spoon the cream into the piping bag and pipe a line of cream on one half of each éclair. Reassemble the éclairs.

Mix the icing sugar and cocoa with about 2 tablespoons of water to make a smooth icing. Spread this over the tops of the éclairs and sprinkle the chopped hazelnuts on top.

As these éclairs contain fresh cream, they should be stored in the refrigerator until serving and are best eaten on the day they are made.

Cherry pies
makes 24 pies

These mini cherry pies are bursting with tangy fruit, encased in a rich, buttery pastry.
They are especially good served warm with ice cream. If you are short of time, you can use
ready-made cherry pie filling with a little extra lemon juice stirred through.

PREPARATION: 30 MINUTES | BAKING: 15–20 MINUTES | CHILLING: 1 HOUR

for the filling
450g cherries, pitted and stems removed
120g caster sugar
juice of 1 lemon
1 tablespoon butter
1 tablespoon cornflour

for the pastry
180g butter
380g plain flour, plus extra for dusting
120g caster sugar, plus extra for sprinkling
2 egg yolks
icing sugar for dusting

equipment
two 12-hole bun tins, greased; 9cm round,
fluted-edge biscuit cutter; small heart cutter

Begin by preparing the cherry filling, as this
needs to cool before you make the pies. Place
the cherries, sugar and 3 tablespoons of water in
a saucepan and bring them to a simmer on the
Boiling Plate. Add the lemon juice. Simmer
until the cherries are soft and the juice is syrupy,
then add the butter. Mix the cornflour with one
tablespoon of the cherry juice and then stir this
into the cherries. Cook on the Boiling Plate for
a few minutes until the sauce has thickened.
Leave aside to cool.

For the pastry, rub the butter into the flour with
your fingertips. Add the caster sugar and egg
yolks plus about 3 or 4 tablespoons of cold water
and use your hands to bring everything together
into a soft dough, dusting the mixture with a
little extra flour if it is too sticky. Wrap the pastry
in cling film and chill in the fridge for one hour.

On a flour-dusted surface, roll out half the pastry
thinly using a rolling pin. Cut out 24 rounds of
pastry using the biscuit cutter. Place one pastry
round in each hole of the bun tin and press

down with your fingers. Place a spoonful of
the cherry mixture in the centre of each pie.
Roll out the remaining pastry and cut out
24 more circles, but this time cut a small heart
shape out of the centre, re-rolling the pastry as
necessary; place one circle of top of each pie.
Pinch the edges with your fingers to make a
pretty patterned edge and to seal the pastry.

Bake in the Roasting Oven on the middle
runners for 10 minutes, then cover with a cold
shelf and cook for a further 5 minutes until the
pastry is golden brown (or transfer to the Baking
Oven). Watch carefully towards the end of
cooking, for if the cherry filling gets too hot
it will bubble up over the pastry.

Leave the pies to cool in the tins for 20 minutes,
then remove from the tins and cool completely
on a rack. Dust with icing sugar to serve.

The pies can be stored for up to 3 days in an
airtight container.

Limoncello cream slices
makes 12

These dainty pastry slices are quick and easy to prepare. Filled with lemon curd and a limoncello cream, they are the perfect tangy treat to serve with glasses of chilled limoncello, the Italian drink of choice on the Amalfi coast.

PREPARATION: 15 MINUTES | BAKING: 10–15 MINUTES

500g puff pastry
milk for brushing
caster sugar for sprinkling
1 tablespoon limoncello
200ml double cream
4 tablespoons lemon curd
icing sugar for dusting

equipment
baking sheet; 8cm triangle biscuit cutter; piping bag fitted with a large star nozzle

Dust a clean work surface with flour and roll out the pastry to 5mm thickness. Cut out 24 triangles of pastry, using the cutter, and place on the baking tray. Brush each triangle with a little milk and sprinkle with caster sugar.

Bake the triangles on the middle shelf of the Roasting Oven for 5 minutes, turn the tray and bake for a further 5–10 minutes until the pastry has risen and is golden brown. Cover with a cold shelf if the pastry starts to brown too much. Remove from the oven and leave to cool on the tray.

For the filling, add the limoncello to the cream and whip to stiff peaks. Spoon the cream into the piping bag and pipe stars of cream on 12 of the pastry triangles. Top with a little lemon curd and then place a second triangle on top. Dust with icing sugar before serving.

These slices need to be kept in the refrigerator, as they contain fresh cream, and are best eaten on the day they are made.

Cakes, Roulades & Rolls

Victoria sponge with strawberry jam

serves 10

The delicate Victoria sponge is the most classic of teatime cakes. Filled here with whipped cream and strawberry jam, this cake is the perfect centrepiece for any tea party.

280g butter or margarine
280g caster sugar
5 eggs
280g self-raising flour
1 teaspoon baking powder
1 heaped tablespoon soured cream
1 teaspoon vanilla extract

for the filling
300ml double cream, whipped to stiff peaks
strawberry jam (see below)
300g strawberries

for dusting
icing sugar

equipment
two 20cm round, deep sandwich tins, greased and lined (see page 8); piping bag fitted with large star nozzle

For the cake, cream together the butter and sugar until light and creamy. Beat in the eggs, one at a time. Sift in the flour and baking powder and fold in the soured cream and vanilla.

Spoon the mixture into the cake tins and spread out evenly. Bake on the bottom runners of the Roasting Oven below a cold shelf (or in the Baking Oven) for 20–25 minutes until the cakes are golden brown and spring back to your touch and when a clean skewer inserted into the centre comes out clean. Turn the cakes on to a rack to cool.

When you are ready to serve, place one cake on a serving plate. Spoon the cream into the piping bag and pipe stars of cream in concentric circles to cover the top of the cake. Spoon a generous amount of strawberry jam over the cream

(a meanly filled sponge cake is never good). Remove the top from all the strawberries (reserving a few whole ones to place on top of the cake) and cut into slices. Place on top of the jam. Top with the second cake. Dust the cake with icing sugar and arrange a few strawberries on top to serve.

This cake should ideally be eaten straight away or stored in the refrigerator, as it contains fresh cream. It will keep for 2 days if refrigerated.

Strawberry jam

Quick and easy to prepare, this jam is best made with ripe and flavourful strawberries. Jam sugar contains pectin, and using this reduces the cooking time needed for the jam to set, so in no time at all you will have perfect strawberry jam!

makes 2 jars

1kg jam sugar
800g strawberries, hulled
juice of 1 lemon
1 vanilla pod
1 tablespoon butter

Place the sugar in a heatproof bowl and warm in the Simmering Oven for 20 minutes; this helps the sugar to dissolve. Place the strawberries in a jam pan (or large saucepan), add the warmed sugar and lemon juice, and mash with a potato masher. Split the vanilla pod in half with a sharp knife

and remove the seeds using the back of the knife. Add the seeds and the vanilla pod to the pan.

Place the pan on the Boiling Plate and bring to the boil; leave the jam to boil for about 10 minutes. (Alternatively, the jam can be cooked on the floor of the Roasting Oven for the same length of time.) To test for set, chill a saucer in the freezer and then drop a little of the jam on to it. Press it with your fingertip; a skin should form and wrinkle. If it does not, return the pan to the heat and cook for a few

more minutes, then re-test. Remove any foam from the top of the jam using a spoon. Add the butter and stir until melted.

Leave the jam to cool slightly, then pour into sterilised jars.

The jam can be stored in the refrigerator for up to 3 months until needed.

Carrot and hazelnut cake
serves 10

Carrot cake is one of my all-time favourites, particularly when topped with a cream cheese icing.
This carrot cake has the additional crunch of hazelnuts and juicy sultanas.
I hope you like it as much as I do.

PREPARATION: 25 MINUTES | BAKING: 90 MINUTES

225g butter, softened
115g caster sugar
115g dark brown sugar
4 eggs
225g self-raising flour
225g carrots, peeled and grated
125g chopped, toasted hazelnuts
200ml buttermilk
115g sultanas

for the icing

50g butter, softened
100g cream cheese
1 tablespoon orange juice
200g icing sugar, sifted
chopped, toasted hazelnuts for sprinkling

equipment

23cm round springform tin, greased and lined
(see page 8)

For the cake, cream together the butter, caster sugar and brown sugar until creamy. Beat in the eggs, one at a time. Sift in the flour and fold in, together with the grated carrot, hazelnuts, buttermilk and sultanas.

Spoon the mixture into the cake tin and spread out evenly. Bake in the Roasting Oven below a cold shelf (or in the Baking Oven) for 30 minutes, turning it halfway through cooking. Transfer the cake to the Simmering Oven and cook for a further hour until the cake is golden brown and springs back to your touch and when a skewer inserted into the centre comes out clean. Turn the cake on to a wire rack to cool.

For the icing, whisk together the butter, cream cheese, orange juice and icing sugar to a smooth consistency. Spoon the icing on top of the cake and sprinkle with hazelnuts to serve.

This cake will keep well for up to 3 days stored in an airtight container.

Chocolate cherry cake
serves 10

This is a truly indulgent cake, rich with dark chocolate and studded with fresh cherries. Because it contains no flour, it is gluten free (provided that the icing sugar does not contain a wheat-based anti-caking agent and that the chocolate is also gluten free) and so is a treat that everyone can enjoy.

PREPARATION: 25 MINUTES | BAKING: 30–35 MINUTES

100g butter
250g dark chocolate (70% cocoa solids), chopped
4 eggs, separated
175g icing sugar, sifted, plus extra for dusting
70g white chocolate chips
150g cherries, pitted

to serve
250ml double cream
150g cherries

equipment
23cm round springform tin

Melt the butter and chocolate in a bowl on the black enamel top of the Aga (or on the Warming Plate).

Whisk together the egg yolks and icing sugar until thick and creamy, then fold in the chocolate mixture with a spatula.

Whisk the egg whites to stiff peaks then fold them into the chocolate mixture a third at a time. Fold in the white chocolate chips.

Remove the base of the cake tin (this will not be needed) Place the ring section on top of a double thickness of kitchen foil, each a bit longer than the combined height plus the diameter of the tin, placed at right angles to each other. Press the foil up the sides of the tin and fold it securely over the edge. Grease the bottom foil and the sides of the tin and then spoon in the mixture. Using foil as the bottom of the tin makes it easier to position the cake on the serving plate.

Place on a cold shelf (or an extra-large baking tray) and spoon in the cake mixture. Sprinkle the pitted cherries evenly on top.

Bake the cake in the middle of the Roasting Oven below another cold shelf (or in the Baking Oven) for 30–35 minutes. Remove the cake from the oven and leave in the tin to cool. The cake will still feel soft below the crust but will set on cooling and have a mousse-like texture when cold. Once it has cooled completely, peel back the foil and loosen and remove the sides of the tin. Use the foil to lift the cake on to the serving plate, then carefully pull it away from the bottom of the cake.

When you are ready to serve, whip the cream to stiff peaks and spoon on top of the cake. Decorate with the cherries.

The cake will keep for up to 2 days stored in the refrigerator.

Lemon and lavender yoghurt cake

serves 8

I love to use lavender in cooking – it gives a fragrant perfume to scones and shortbread and also to this delicious lemon drizzle cake. Make sure that you use pesticide-free lavender (which has not been sprayed with any chemicals). It is available from good health food shops, and lavender sugar is now available in some supermarkets.

PREPARATION: 15 MINUTES | BAKING: 25–35 MINUTES

115g butter, softened
115g caster sugar
2 eggs
115g self-raising flour
zest and juice of 2 lemons
80ml natural yoghurt
1 teaspoon culinary lavender
2 tablespoons icing sugar

equipment
loaf tin 8.5 x 22cm, greased and lined (see page 8)

Cream together the butter and sugar. Whisk in the eggs, one at a time. Fold in the flour, lemon zest and yoghurt.

Spoon the mixture into the loaf tin and place on the lowest shelf of the Roasting Oven below a cold shelf (or in the Baking Oven). Cook for 25–35 minutes, turning the tin halfway through cooking, until the cake springs back to your touch and a skewer inserted into the centre comes out clean.

Remove the cake from the oven and leave it to cool in the tin.

While the cake is still warm, heat the lemon juice with the lavender and icing sugar in a saucepan on the Boiling Plate. Bring to the boil and then pour over the cake while it is still in the cake pan. When the cake has cooled, turn it out to serve.

This cake will keep in an airtight container for up to 3 days but is best eaten on the day it is made.

Blackberry and apple cake
serves 10

Ripe juicy blackberries and apples are the quintessential tastes of autumn. This cake has a glazed apple topping, reminiscent of classic French apple tarts, and looks almost too good to cut. If blackberries are not available you can substitute raspberries (fresh or frozen) for a delicious apple and raspberry cake.

PREPARATION: 20 MINUTES | BAKING: 35–40 MINUTES

225g butter, softened
225g caster sugar plus extra for sprinkling
4 eggs
170g self-raising flour, sifted
85g ground almonds
2 tablespoons soured cream
3 dessert apples
juice of 1 lemon

to assemble

2 tablespoons apricot jam
juice of 1 lemon
250g blackberries
300ml double cream, whipped to stiff peaks
blackberry and apple jam or blackberry jelly

equipment

2 loose-bottomed 20cm sandwich cake tins, greased and lined (see page 8); piping bag with large star nozzle (optional)

Whisk together the butter and caster sugar until light and creamy. Add the eggs one at a time, whisking after each is added. Add the flour, ground almonds and soured cream, and fold in gently with a spatula. Spoon the mixture into the prepared cake tin and level using a spatula.

Core the apples and cut into thin slices. Toss the apple slices in the lemon juice and then arrange in rings on the top of each cake. Sprinkle the apple slices with caster sugar. Bake on the bottom runners of the Roasting Oven below a cold shelf (or in the Baking Oven) for 35–40 minutes until the cakes are golden and spring back to your touch and a skewer comes out clean when inserted into the centre.

Turn the cakes out onto a cooling rack, apple side up. Combine the apricot jam and lemon juice in a saucepan and heat gently. Brush this over the top of each cake to glaze. Leave the cakes to cool completely.

When you are ready to serve, place one cake, apple side up, on a serving plate. Spoon the cream into the piping bag and pipe large stars of cream on top of the cake, spacing them evenly. If you don't have a piping bag, you can simply use a spoon to put dollops of cream over the surface. Intersperse the cream stars with the blackberries, and then place spoonfuls of jam on top. Place the second cake on top of the first one.

As the cake contains fresh cream, it needs to be eaten straight away or stored in the refrigerator until serving. It is best eaten on the day it is made but will keep for up to 2 days in a sealed container in the refrigerator.

Sweet Things From the Aga

Spiced honey cake

This cake is flavoured with the delicious scents of chai tea which are infused into the fruit.
Soaked in a honey syrup, this is a good old-fashioned loaf cake, with modern-day spicing.

serves 8

PREPARATION: 20 MINUTES | BAKING: 30–40 MINUTES

1 chai tea bag
150ml water, boiling
150g golden sultanas
115g butter, softened
85g caster sugar
30g clear (runny) honey
2 eggs
115g self-raising flour, sifted
1 tablespoon soured cream

for the drizzle
1 tablespoon clear (runny) honey

equipment
loaf pan 8.5 x 22cm, greased and lined (see page 8)

Place the tea bag in a mug and pour the boiling
water on to it; leave to steep for 4 minutes.
Remove the tea bag, add the sultanas and leave
to infuse for one hour, covered with cling film,
at room temperature.

Whisk together the butter, sugar and honey.
Add the eggs and whisk in. Add the flour and
soured cream and fold in. Drain the sultanas,
reserving the poaching liquid.

Set aside 1 tablespoon of the sultanas and add
the remainder to the cake mixture along with
1 tablespoon of the liquid.

Spoon the mixture into the cake pan and bake
for 30–40 minutes in the Roasting Oven under
a cold shelf (or in the Baking Oven) until the
cake is golden brown and springs back when
you press it with a finger and when a skewer
inserted into the centre comes out clean.

Remove the cake from the oven and leave it to
cool in the tin. Heat the honey for the drizzle
with 1 tablespoon of the reserved chai tea,
spoon this over the cake and decorate with the
reserved sultanas. When the cake is cool release
it from the tin.

The cake can be stored for up to 3 days in an
airtight container.

Pear Belle Hélène cake

serves 6~8

Poires Belle Hélène is a classic French favourite of poached pears, ice cream and chocolate sauce.
It is a dessert with poignant memories for me, as it is the dish that beat me in the final of *MasterChef*.
This is my cake tribute to Steven's Wallis's wonderful pudding – a worthy winner! You can make
this recipe gluten free by substituting gluten-free self-raising flour and ensuring that the chocolate
you use is gluten free; the result will be equally delicious.

PREPARATION: 25 MINUTES | BAKING: 30–40 MINUTES

115g butter, softened
60g dark brown sugar
2 eggs
115g ground almonds
30g self-raising flour
200g plain chocolate, melted
3 ripe pears, peeled, with stem intact

for the sauce

300ml double cream
100g plain chocolate, chopped into a few pieces
1 tablespoon butter
1 tablespoon golden syrup

equipment

Loaf tin 8.5 x 22cm, greased and lined (see page 8)

For the cake, cream together the butter and
sugar until light and creamy. Add the eggs one
at a time, whisking after each. Fold in the
ground almonds, flour and melted chocolate.

Cut each pear in half lengthways, leaving half
a stem on each half, and scoop out the core and
seeds with a teaspoon.

Spoon the chocolate cake mixture into the
prepared tin and then push the six pear halves
into the cake mixture along the middle line
of the cake. Bake on the bottom runners of the
Roasting Oven below a cold shelf (or in the
Baking Oven) for 30–40 minutes until the cake
is firm and a skewer into the centre comes out
clean. Leave the cake to cool completely in
the tin.

For the sauce, place the cream, chopped
chocolate, butter and syrup in a saucepan and
heat on the Simmering Plate for a few minutes
until the butter and chocolate have melted.
Serve slices of cake with the warm chocolate
sauce, adding a scoop of vanilla ice cream for
an extra treat, if you wish.

Raspberry and lemon roulade
serves 10

This light and lemony dessert is ideal for a summer's day. The sponge melts in the mouth and the tangy raspberries and lemon curd perfectly complement the whipped cream.

PREPARATION: 30 MINUTES | BAKING: 10–15 MINUTES

150ml milk
40g plain flour
5 eggs, separated
140g caster sugar
zest of 2 lemons
50g flaked almonds

for the filling

350ml double cream
225g fresh raspberries
4 tablespoons lemon curd
icing sugar for dusting

equipment

38 x 28cm baking tin, greased and lined
  (see page 8)

Heat the milk and flour together in a saucepan on the Simmering Plate, then whisk to a smooth paste, then leave to cool.

Whisk the egg yolks and caster sugar together until thick and creamy. Beat in the flour mixture. Whip the egg whites to stiff peaks and fold into the egg yolk mixture, a third at a time, together with the lemon zest.

Pour the mixture into the prepared tin and spread out evenly. Sprinkle the nuts on top. Bake on the bottom runners of the Roasting Oven for 7 minutes, then turn the tray and bake for a further 5–8 minutes until the sponge is golden brown. If the sponge starts to brown too much, place a cold shelf over it. (If available, the Baking Oven can be used.)

Lay a sheet of baking parchment larger than the tin on a flat surface. Dust with icing sugar. Remove the roulade from the oven and turn out, upside down, on top of the sugar-dusted sheet. Cover with a clean, damp tea towel and leave for 15 minutes. Remove the towel and the lining paper and roll the roulade up from one of the short ends, so that the sugar-dusted paper ends up rolled through the sponge. Leave to cool completely.

When you are ready to serve, whip the double cream to stiff peaks. Unroll the roulade and, using a spatula, spread a layer of cream over the cake. Add the raspberries and spoon the lemon curd on top. Using your hands, roll up the roulade.

Place the roulade on a serving plate and dust with a little extra icing sugar. Serve straight away.

Alternatively the roulade can be stored in the refrigerator (as it contains fresh cream), for up to 1 day.

Tropical roulade
serves 10

Rum, pineapple, coconut – all the elements of one of my favourite cocktails, piña colada – are wrapped up in this creamy roulade. Sunshine on a plate!

for the cake
150ml milk
40g plain flour
5 eggs, separated
140g caster sugar
50g coconut cream

for the filling
1 small ripe pineapple
100ml coconut rum
juice of 1 lime
350ml double cream
50g coconut cream
3 tablespoons flaked coconut

for the topping
flaked coconut, toasted, for sprinkling
icing sugar for dusting

equipment
38 x 28cm baking tin, greased and lined
   (see page 8); silicon-mat-lined baking tray

Peel the pineapple and cut off 4 very thin slices. Place on a baking tray lined with a silicon mat and cook in the Simmering Oven for about 1 hour until crisp and dried. Core and chop the remaining pineapple for the filling and cut into small chunks. Place in a bowl and pour over the coconut rum and lime juice. Cover with cling film and leave to chill in the refrigerator until you are ready to serve.

For the roulade, heat the milk and flour together in a saucepan on the Simmering Plate up to the simmering point, then whisk to a smooth paste.

Whisk the egg yolks, caster sugar and coconut cream together until thick and creamy. Beat in the flour mixture.

Whip the egg whites to stiff peaks; fold into the egg yolk mixture, a third at a time.

Pour the mixture into the prepared tin and spread out evenly. Sprinkle the coconut on top and bake on the bottom runners of the Roasting Oven for 7 minutes, then turn the tray and bake for a further 5–8 minutes until the sponge is golden brown. If the sponge starts to brown too much place a cold shelf over it. (If available, the Baking Oven can be used.)

Lay a sheet of baking parchment larger than the tin on a flat surface. Dust with icing sugar. Remove the roulade from the oven and turn out, upside down, on top of the icing sugar. Cover with a clean, damp tea towel and leave for 15 minutes. Remove the towel and the lining paper from the roulade and roll the cake up from one of the short ends, so that the sugar-covered parchment ends up rolled through the sponge. Leave to cool completely.

When you are ready to serve, whip the double cream and coconut cream together to stiff peaks. Unroll the roulade and remove the parchment. Trim away any untidy edges. Using a spatula, spread a layer of cream over the cake and then top with slices of pineapple. Using your hands, roll up the roulade.

Place the roulade on a serving plate and top with the dried pineapple slices. Serve straight away.

Alternatively, the roulade can be stored in the refrigerator (as it contains fresh cream), for up to 2 days.

Banana roulade

serves 10

This indulgent roulade contains both fresh bananas and a banana chip crumb topping, and is served with a creamy caramel sauce and whipped cream. It is a sure-fire winner for all banana lovers.

PREPARATION: 30 MINUTES | BAKING: 10–15 MINUTES

150ml milk
40g self-raising flour
1 ripe banana
140g dark brown sugar
5 eggs, separated
zest of 1 lemon

for the crumb topping

50g sun-dried banana chips
icing sugar, sieved, for dusting

for the caramel sauce

60g caster sugar, plus 60g dark brown sugar
60g butter
180ml double cream
1 tablespoon golden syrup

to assemble

300ml double cream
2 ripe bananas
juice of 1 lemon

equipment

baking tin 38 x 28cm, greased and lined
   (see page 8)

For the sponge, heat the milk and flour together in a saucepan on the Simmering Plate and whisk to a smooth paste, then leave to cool. Peel the banana and crush it with a fork. Put the banana in a mixing bowl, along with the sugar and egg yolks, and whisk until thick and creamy. Beat in the flour mixture.

Whip the egg whites to stiff peaks. Fold into the egg yolk mixture, a third at a time, together with the lemon zest. Pour the mixture into the prepared tin and spread out evenly. Bake on the bottom runners of the Roasting Oven for 7 minutes then turn the tray and bake for a further 5–8 minutes until the sponge is golden brown. If it starts to brown too much, place a cold shelf over it.

While the cake is baking, prepare the crumb topping. Lay a sheet of baking parchment larger than the cake tin on a flat surface. Blitz the banana chips to a fine crumb in a food processor and sprinkle evenly over the sheet (reserving a tablespoonful of the crumbs for decoration). Dust the sheet liberally with the sieved icing sugar.

Remove the roulade from the oven and turn it out, upside down, on top of the banana crumbs. Cover it with a clean, damp tea towel and leave for 15 minutes. Remove the towel and the lining parchment from the roulade and roll it up from one of the short ends, so that the banana-covered paper ends up rolled through the sponge. Leave to cool completely.

For the caramel sauce, place the caster sugar and brown sugar in a saucepan with the butter, double cream and golden syrup and cook on the Simmering Plate until the sugar and butter have melted and you have a smooth caramel sauce. Set aside to cool.

When you are ready to serve, whip the double cream to stiff peaks. Unroll the roulade. Using a spatula, spread a layer of cream over the cake. Peel the bananas and cut into slices, toss lightly in the lemon juice, drain, and then place on top of the cream. Drizzle with several spoonfuls of the caramel sauce, then, using your hands, roll up the roulade.

Place the roulade on a serving plate, drizzle with a little of the caramel sauce and top with the reserved banana crumbs. Serve with the remaining caramel sauce on the side.

The roulade can be stored in the refrigerator (as it contains fresh cream) for a few hours, but is best eaten on the day it is made.

Sweet Things From the Aga

Swiss roll

serves 8

The first recipe I made in my cookery classes at school, when I was nine years old, was a Swiss roll. So simple to make, yet this delicate sponge and jam, lightly dusted with caster sugar, is utterly delicious!

PREPARATION: 10 MINUTES | BAKING: 8–10 MINUTES

4 large eggs
1 teaspoon vanilla extract
115g caster sugar, plus extra for sprinkling
115g self-raising flour
1 teaspoon baking powder
6 tablespoons strawberry jam

equipment
Swiss roll pan 35 x 25cm, greased and lined
  (see page 8)

In a large mixing bowl, whisk together the eggs, vanilla and caster sugar for about 5 minutes, using an electric mixer, until the mixture is very thick, creamy and pale.

Sift together the flour and baking powder and fold into the egg mixture with a spatula. Fold very gently, otherwise you will lose all the air whipped into the eggs, which gives the roll its light texture.

Spoon the mixture into the Swiss roll pan and bake on the bottom runners of the Roasting Oven for 5 minutes, then turn the tray around and cook for a further 3–5 minutes until the sponge is golden brown and feels just firm to your touch. Cover with a cold shelf if the sponge starts to brown too much.

Sprinkle a generous amount of caster sugar onto a sheet of baking parchment. Turn the sponge out on to the caster-sugar-dusted sheet and cover with a clean, damp tea towel. Leave it for 5 minutes, then remove the towel and lining paper. Trim away the edges of the sponge using a sharp knife. Mix the jam with a spoon so that it is easily spreadable and spread it over the sponge.

Roll up the sponge from one of the short ends, using the sugar-dusted baking parchment to guide the sponge as you roll. Leave the Swiss roll wrapped in the baking parchment until cool. Turn it out on to a plate to serve and dust with a little extra caster sugar if desired.

This cake is best served on the day it is made but it will keep for up to 2 days in an airtight container.

Mocha Swiss roll

serves 8

A caffeine hit with chocolate and whipped cream makes this light Swiss roll the
perfect morning coffee treat.

PREPARATION: 25 MINUTES | BAKING: ABOUT 10 MINUTES

for the roll

4 large eggs
1 teaspoon vanilla extract

115g caster sugar, plus extra for sprinkling
1 tablespoon espresso coffee
115g self-raising flour
1 teaspoon baking powder
cocoa and icing sugar, for dusting

for the filling

300ml double cream
1 tablespoon coffee liqueur
1 tablespoon espresso coffee
2 tablespoons cocoa
3 tablespoons chocolate curls or coarsely grated
   chocolate
30g plain chocolate melted
12 chocolate coffee beans

equipment

Swiss roll pan 35 x 25cm, greased and lined
   (see page 8); piping bag fitted with a star nozzle

In a large mixing bowl, whisk together the
eggs, vanilla, caster sugar and coffee for about
5 minutes, using an electric mixer, until the
mixture is very thick, creamy and pale.

Sift together the flour and baking powder and
fold into the egg mixture with a spatula. Fold
very gently, otherwise you will lose all the air
whipped into the eggs, which gives the roll its
light texture.

Spoon the mixture into the Swiss roll pan and
bake on the bottom runners of the Roasting
Oven for 5 minutes, then turn the tray around
and cook for a further 3–5 minutes until the
sponge is golden brown and feels just firm to
your touch. Cover with a cold shelf if the
sponge starts to brown too much.

Dust a sheet of baking parchment with cocoa
and icing sugar using a sieve and turn the sponge
out onto it upside down and cover with a clean,
damp tea towel. Leave until cool, then remove
the towel and lining paper. Trim away the edges
of the sponge using a sharp knife.

Whisk the cream, coffee liqueur and espresso
together with a whisk until the cream holds stiff
peaks. Spread two-thirds of the cream over the
sponge, dust with cocoa using a sieve and sprinkle
with the chocolate curls. Roll up the sponge
from one of the short ends, using the baking
parchment to guide the sponge as you roll.

Place the roll on a serving plate. Using a spoon,
drizzle thin lines of melted chocolate over the
roll. Spoon the reserved filling into the piping
bag and pipe 10 large stars on top of the roll.
Top each star with a chocolate coffee bean.

Because the roll contains fresh cream it should
be served straight away or stored in the
refrigerator until you are ready to eat it, for
up to 1 day.

Sweet Things From the Aga

Puddings, Tarts
& Delicious Desserts

Pistachio pithivier

serves 8

There is something about a pithivier tart that is really surprising. It is rather ordinary-looking from the outside, but when you cut in to it you are greeted with a gooey, nutty, buttery filling. This is my recipe for pistachio pithivier, but you can substitute any other nuts that you like; almonds or pecans also work well.

PREPARATION: 20 MINUTES | BAKING: 20–25 MINUTES

60g butter
115g icing sugar
115g shelled pistachios
2 egg yolks
2 tablespoons amaretto liqueur
500g puff pastry

for the glaze
1 egg
2 tablespoons icing sugar, plus extra for dusting

equipment
cold shelf lined with baking parchment or a
silicone mat

Begin by making the filling. Cream the butter with the icing sugar. Blitz the pistachios to fine crumbs in a food processor. Add the egg yolks, amaretto and ground pistachios to the butter mixture and whisk together.

Cut the puff pastry in half and roll out each half thinly. Cut out a circle 26cm in diameter from each pastry half. It is easiest to do this by cutting around the edge of a dinner plate using a sharp knife, which will produce a perfect circle.

Place one circle on the prepared baking tray. Spoon the pistachio filling into the middle of the circle and spread out, leaving a 3cm margin around the edge of the pastry. Wet the edge of the pastry circle with water, using a pastry brush, and top with the second circle of pastry. Press the edges down to seal tightly and crimp together with a fork or your fingers.

Whisk together the egg and icing sugar and brush this over the top of the pie. Using a sharp knife score patterns on the top of the pastry, being careful not to cut through to the filling. Bake on the bottom runners of the Roasting Oven for 10 minutes, then cover with a cold shelf and bake for a further 10–15 minutes (or use the Baking Oven). Dust with icing sugar and serve warm or cold.

The pithivier can be stored for up to 2 days in an airtight container but is best eaten on the day it is made.

Sweet Things From the Aga

Chocolate pecan pie
serves 10

I love the classic American dessert pecan pie – rich, buttery pastry, crunchy nuts and a sticky toffee sauce. My version has a hint of chocolate in the pastry, and it is always popular with friends and family when I serve it.

PREPARATION: 30 MINUTES | CHILLING: 1 HOUR | BAKING: 15–25 MINUTES

for the pastry

115g butter, chilled
240g plain flour, sifted, plus extra for dusting
40g cocoa, sifted
40g caster sugar
2 egg yolks

for the filling

400g pecan nuts
150g caster sugar
150g dark brown sugar
2 teaspoons cinnamon
2 teaspoons vanilla extract
100g butter
7 tablespoons golden syrup
3 eggs

equipment

26cm round loose-bottomed tart tin; food processor

For the chocolate pastry, rub the butter into the flour and cocoa with your fingertips. Add the sugar and egg yolks and bring together into a soft dough, adding 1 or 2 tablespoons of cold water if needed.

Wrap the pastry in cling film and chill it in the refrigerator for 30 minutes. On a flour-dusted surface roll the pastry out thinly; transfer it to the tin using the rolling pin. Press the pastry down into the pan, trim the edges and prick with a fork. Chill the tin in the refrigerator for 30 minutes.

For the filling, blitz half of the pecans to fine crumbs in the food processor and pour into the chilled pastry case. Heat the caster sugar, brown sugar, cinnamon, vanilla, butter and golden syrup in a saucepan on the Simmering Plate until the sugar and butter have melted. Set aside to cool.

Beat the eggs and whisk them into the cooled syrup. Pass the syrup through a sieve and pour most of it over the chopped pecans, reserving a little for glazing. Place rings of whole pecans on top of the filling for a decorative effect. Bake in the Roasting Oven for 15–25 minutes on the bottom shelf, covered with a cold shelf if necessary (or in the Baking Oven), until the pie is set, but with a slight wobble. Remove the pie from the oven and brush the remaining syrup over the surface to glaze. Leave the pie to cool before serving.

The pie will keep well for up to 3 days stored in an airtight container.

Rhubarb custard tart

serves 10

Custard tart is one of my favourites – rich and creamy with hints of nutmeg.
Although the classic version is delicious, the addition of poached rhubarb adds a new
dimension to this tart, reminiscent of childhood favourite rhubarb and custard sweets.
Make this with first-of-the-season rhubarb for best results.

**PREPARATION: 30 MINUTES | BAKING: ABOUT 1¹/₄ HOURS |
CHILLING: 1¹/₂ HOURS**

for the pastry

115g butter, chilled
280g plain flour, sifted, plus extra for dusting
¹/₄ teaspoon salt

for the poached rhubarb

450g rhubarb
50g caster sugar

for the filling

6 free-range egg yolks
70g caster sugar
350ml double cream
1 teaspoon vanilla extract

equipment

ovenproof dish approximately 25cm in diameter;
   26cm flan dish, greased; baking parchment;
   baking beans

Peel and chop the rhubarb into 5cm lengths.
Place in the ovenproof dish, sprinkle with the
caster sugar and add 2 tablespoons of water.
Bake for 10–15 minutes in the Roasting Oven
until soft but still holding its shape. Leave to
cool, then drain away any liquid.

For the pastry, put the flour and salt into a
mixing bowl and rub the butter in, using your
hands, until it resembles coarse breadcrumbs.
Add 1 or 2 tablespoons of cold water and mix in
with a round-bladed knife, adding a little more
water if the mixture is too dry. Wrap the pastry
in cling film and chill in the refrigerator for
1 hour.

On a flour-dusted surface, roll out the pastry
thinly and line the flan dish with it. Press the
pastry in firmly with your fingers and trim away
any excess using a sharp knife. Prick the base
with a fork and chill in the refrigerator for a
further 30 minutes.

Line the pastry with baking parchment, fill
with baking beans and bake blind for about
10–15 minutes on the middle runners of the
Roasting Oven until the pastry is golden brown.

Distribute the rhubarb evenly in the tart shell.
Whisk together the yolks and caster sugar until
light and creamy. Slowly pour in the cream and
vanilla and whisk everything together. Pour into
a jug and then slowly pour into the tart shell.

Bake the tart for 40 minutes in the bottom of
the Simmering Oven, then move to the top of
the Simmering Oven and cook for a further
30 minutes until the top of the tart is light
golden brown and set but with a slight wobble.
Chill before serving.

The tart can be stored in the refrigerator for up
to 2 days.

Raspberry meringue pie
serves 8

When I was a child, lemon meringue pie was one of my favourite desserts. I may be biased, but my mum makes the best-ever lemon meringue pie, and I always ask for it when we have lunch at her house. Inspired by that delicacy, I've created this raspberry meringue pie, with its bright pink filling nestled beneath airy meringue.

PREPARATION: 30 MINUTES | BAKING: ABOUT 1 HOUR | CHILLING: 1 HOUR

for the pastry
90g butter
190g plain flour
60g caster sugar
1 egg yolk

for the filling
250g caster sugar
450g raspberries
40g cornflour
2 egg yolks

for the meringue
5 egg whites
6 tablespoons caster sugar

equipment
26cm round-bottomed tart tin, greased; baking parchment; baking beans

For the pastry, rub the butter into the flour using your fingers until it resembles breadcrumbs. Add the sugar, egg yolk and 1 or 2 tablespoons of cold water and mix in with a palette knife, adding a little more water if the mixture is too dry. Wrap the pastry in cling film and chill in the refrigerator for 30 minutes.

On a flour-dusted surface, roll out the pastry thinly and line the tart tin with it, pressing in tightly with your fingertips and trimming away any excess pastry with a sharp knife. Prick the base with a fork and chill in the refrigerator for a further 30 minutes.

Line the pastry with baking parchment, fill with baking beans and bake blind for about 10 minutes in the Roasting Oven until the pastry is golden brown, covering with a cold shelf if needed.

For the raspberry curd filling, heat the sugar with 250ml water on the Boiling Plate until the sugar has dissolved. Add the raspberries to the pan and simmer for about 5 minutes until the fruit is soft. Strain through a sieve to remove the raspberry seeds and leave to cool slightly.

Add some of the warm raspberry liquid to the cornflour and mix well. Beat the egg yolks into the cornflour mixture and pour back into the pan. Heat on the Boiling Plate for a few minutes until the raspberry liquid thickens, whisking all the time.

Remove from the heat, strain and leave to cool, then pour into the baked pastry case.

In a clean bowl, whisk the egg whites to stiff peaks and then add the caster sugar a spoonful at a time, until you have a smooth, glossy meringue that holds its shape when you lift the beaters. Spoon the meringue on top of the raspberry filling.

Bake in the Roasting Oven on the bottom runners for 5 minutes, then cover with a cold shelf and cook for a further 10 minutes. Transfer to the middle runners of the Simmering Oven and cook for a further 45 minutes until the meringue is crisp but still soft inside. Leave to cool, then chill in the refrigerator before serving.

The pie can be stored in the refrigerator for up to 2 days.

Orange caramel choux buns
makes 12 buns

These delicate choux buns make a spectacular centrepiece dessert decorated with silver dragees, spun sugar and gold leaf. At French weddings, a huge cone-shaped structure of these choux buns, called a *croquembouche*, is the preferred alternative to a wedding cake. Spun sugar may look complicated, but with a little practice it is actually easy to prepare.

PREPARATION: 40 MINUTES | BAKING: ABOUT 20 MINUTES

for the pastry
65g plain flour
50g butter
2 eggs

for the patisserie cream
1 tablespoon cornflour
60g caster sugar
1 egg and 1 egg yolk
100ml milk
150ml double cream
1 teaspoon orange zest
3 tablespoons orange curd

to assemble
100g caster sugar
silver chocolate dragees
edible gold leaf

equipment
Baking sheets, greased and lined; piping bag
   fitted with a medium round nozzle

First, make the pastry by sieving the flour twice to remove any lumps. Heat the butter in a saucepan with 150ml water on the Boiling Plate until the butter is melted, bring to the boil, then quickly add the sifted flour all at once and remove from the heat. Beat hard with a wooden spoon or whisk until the dough forms a ball and no longer sticks to the sides of the pan. Leave to cool for about 5 minutes.

Whisk the eggs together and then beat into the pastry, a small amount at a time, using a balloon whisk. The mixture will form a sticky paste which holds its shape when you lift the whisk up.

Spoon the pastry into the piping bag and pipe 12 balls on to the baking sheets, a small distance apart. Wet your finger and smooth down any peaks from the piping so that the balls are round.

Bake on the middle runners of the Roasting Oven for about 15 minutes until crisp, then with a sharp knife cut a small slit into each ball and return to the oven for 5 minutes until crisp. If the pastry starts to brown too much, cover with a cold shelf. Cool on a rack and then cut a slit into each that will fit the size of your icing nozzle.

To prepare the patisserie cream, whisk together the cornflour, sugar, egg and egg yolk in a bowl until creamy. Place the milk, cream and orange zest in a saucepan and bring to the boil on the Boiling Plate. Pour this over the egg mixture, whisking all the time.

Return the cream to the pan and cook on the Boiling Plate for a few minutes until thick. Pass through a sieve and let cool. Fold in the orange curd and spoon into the piping bag. Pipe the cream into each of the choux buns. Arrange the buns in a stack on a serving plate.

For the caramel topping, heat the caster sugar in a heavy-based saucepan on the Boiling Plate. Do not stir the sugar but swirl the pan to prevent it from burning. The sugar will start to caramelise. You need to watch it carefully at this stage, as it can very quickly turn dark and burn. Once the caramel is a golden colour, remove it from the heat.

Drizzle some of the hot caramel over the tops of the buns to fix them in place.

To prepare the spun sugar, dip a fork into the sugar and pull it away from the pan to make long, fine caramel strands. In order to do this the sugar syrup needs to be just tacky. If it is too hot, the sugar will not cool in the air and create the long, sugary threads you need. If the sugar

sets too much, just return it to the heat for a few seconds and then make more sugar threads. For an even more impressive effect, decorate the choux buns with a little gold leaf. Once you have made the sugar strands, drape them over the buns.

The choux buns should be eaten on the day they are made; however, they can be arranged and refrigerated until you are nearly ready to serve, when you should make the spun sugar.

Rice pudding
serves 8

I can honestly say that until I made it in the Aga, rice pudding was not one of my favourite desserts. I am sure this comes of being served with frogspawn-like versions at school when I was little. This pudding is, however, altogether different; utterly indulgent with butter and sweetened with condensed milk, it has an almost caramel flavour. A little girl in my village called Rafaela (who assured me she didn't like rice pudding) tried this and was an instant convert!

PREPARATION: 15 MINUTES | BAKING: 3–4 HOURS

125ml condensed milk
100g butter
120g pudding rice
700ml milk
250ml double cream

equipment
2-litre Aga-proof dish

Heat the condensed milk and butter in a heavy-based saucepan on the Boiling Plate, stirring constantly. When the butter has melted, add the rice and cook for a few minutes until the sauce starts to caramelise and turn golden brown. Take care that it does not burn. Add the milk and cream to the pan, remove from the heat and stir. Don't worry if there are any lumps, as these will disappear during the baking.

Pour the pudding into the dish and cook in the Simmering Oven for about 3 hours until the rice is tender and almost all of the liquid has been absorbed. The exact time will depend on the temperature of your oven, so check it from about $2^1/_2$ hours and then for every 20 minutes or so thereafter. Serve warm.

Ideally the pudding should be eaten straight away; but any left over can be stored in the refrigerator up to 2 days and gently reheated.

Sweet Things From the Aga

Ginger brulées
serves 6

These delicate set custards, flavoured with ginger and topped with a burnt sugar crust that gives the classic 'crack' when you tap into it with a spoon, are one of my favourite desserts. They always bring back memories of childhood holidays in France when we were young. If you wish, you can substitute a split vanilla pod or a teaspoon of ground culinary lavender for the ginger.

**PREPARATION: 20 MINUTES |
COOKING: APPROXIMATELY 10 MINUTES PLUS 3 HOURS CHILLING**

4 balls of stem ginger preserved in syrup
600ml double cream
5 egg yolks
80g caster sugar, plus extra for sprinkling

equipment
6 ramekins or pretty teacups; stand mixer
    (optional); chef's blowtorch (optional)

Finely slice the preserved ginger and place it in a saucepan with the cream. Heat on the Boiling Plate, stirring constantly until the cream starts to boil. Remove from the heat and leave to infuse for 30 minutes.

Whisk the egg yolks and caster sugar together in a mixing bowl until thick, creamy and very pale yellow. Strain the cream through a sieve to remove the ginger pieces and return the cream to the pan. Bring to the boil again and, while whisking, pour the hot cream in a steady stream into the egg mixture. It is easiest to do this using a stand mixer; if you do not have one, ask someone to pour the cream mixture while you whisk the egg mixture.

Return the custard to the pan and heat on the Simmering Plate, whisking all the time, until it starts to thicken. Take care not to overheat the custard as it will curdle. Pour the custard into the ramekins and leave to cool, then transfer to the refrigerator for at least 3 hours to set.

When you are ready to serve, sprinkle the top of each custard with a thin layer of caster sugar and caramelise with a chef's blowtorch. If you haven't got a blowtorch you can heat some sugar in a pan until caramelised (see the recipe for Orange Caramel Choux Buns, page 128) and spoon this over the top in a thin layer once it has cooled slightly.

The brulées will store well in the refrigerator without their sugar topping for up to 3 days. You need to sprinkle and blowtorch the crust at the last minute to prevent the sugar from softening and losing its crispness.

Chocolate toffee pots
makes 6

These little baked pots are rich and indulgent, swirled with dark chocolate and hints of lemon and caramel. You can substitute melted white chocolate for the plain chocolate, if you like, and add a few raspberries to the base of each dish in place of the caramel, for equally delicious results.

PREPARATION: 20 MINUTES | BAKING: 1 HOUR | CHILLING: 3 HOURS

for the chocolate mixture
100g plain chocolate
300g cream cheese, at room temperature
200ml crème fraîche
70g caster sugar
2 small eggs
zest of 1 lemon

for the caramel sauce
50g caster sugar
30g butter
120ml double cream

to decorate
3 tablespoons chocolate curls

equipment
6 small preserving jars; large roasting pan

Begin by making the caramel sauce. Heat the sugar and butter in a saucepan on the Boiling Plate until the sugar starts to caramelise. Remove from the heat, allow to cool slightly, then add the cream. Return to the heat and stir until the sauce is smooth.

Spoon the caramel sauce into the jars. Half-fill a large roasting pan with water and place the jars in the tray.

Melt the chocolate in a bowl on top of the Aga.

Whisk together the cream cheese, crème fraîche, sugar, eggs and lemon zest until smooth and creamy. Drizzle the melted chocolate into the mixture and stir through very gently with a spatula for a rippled effect.

Pour the chocolate and cheese mixture into the jars on top of the caramel. Transfer the roasting pan to the bottom runners of the Roasting Oven with a cold shelf above (or into the Baking Oven) and bake for 20 minutes. Transfer the pan to the Simmering Oven and bake for a further 40–50 minutes until set but with a slight wobble in the centre.

When the puddings are cooked, remove them from the oven. Leave the pots to cool and then chill in the refrigerator for at least 3 hours before serving. To serve, sprinkle the chocolate curls on top of each pot.

These pots will keep in the refrigerator for up to 3 days.

Sweet Things From the Aga

Orange crème caramel
serves 6-8

Smooth orange set cream topped with burnt caramel, this is a citrus twist on the classic French crème caramel. The art of a good crème caramel is to cook it very gently and not overheat, which will cause the cream to curdle. The Aga's Simmering Oven is ideal for this.

PREPARATION: 20 MINUTES | BAKING: 3 HOURS | CHILLING: 2 HOURS

for the caramel
150g caster sugar

for the custard
120g caster sugar
4 eggs plus 2 egg yolks
350ml milk
200ml double cream
zest of one orange

equipment
19/20cm crème caramel mould or dish; roasting pan or casserole dish for water bath

Begin by heating the sugar for the caramel, along with 3 tablespoons of water, in a heavy-based saucepan on the Boiling Plate. Heat until the sugar has dissolved and the caramel turns dark, taking care that it does not burn. Pour into the mould or dish. Fit the mould lid or cover tightly with foil.

For the custard, whisk together the sugar, eggs and egg yolks. Add the milk, cream and orange zest, and whisk again. Pour into the mould on top of the caramel.

Place the caramel mould into the roasting (or other large) pan and pour boiling water around it up to three-quarters of the way up the mould. Cook in the Simmering Oven for about 3 hours until the custard is set but with a slight wobble.

Remove the pan from the oven, lift out the mould and leave it to cool, then chill in the fridge for at least 2 hours or overnight.

To unmould, place the caramel mould in a bowl of hot water nearly up to the edge for a few moments, then lift it out; the caramel should have come away slightly from the sides of the mould. Repeat if necessary. (Alternatively, wrap a hot, wet tea towel around the mould for a few moments.) Place a plate on top of the mould and invert the plate and mould together, taking care that the caramel syrup does not spill. It is best to unmould the caramel just before serving.

The custard can be stored for up to 2 days in the refrigerator.

Cherry roly-poly
serves 6

The classic jam roly-poly – made of buttery suet dough and oozing with jam – has long graced our dining tables as a hearty winter pudding. One of the earliest-known varieties is the Bedfordshire clanger – with jam rolled at one end and meat at the other – a farmer's true packed lunch, sweet and savoury all in one. Thankfully my version doesn't contain any meat, just tangy cherries, and is perfect served with lashings of hot custard.

PREPARATION: 20 MINUTES | COOKING: APPROXIMATELY 2 HOURS

for the pastry
225g self-raising flour, sifted
100g suet
1 teaspoon baking powder
$1/_2$ teaspoon salt
1 tablespoon caster sugar
80ml milk

for the filling
250g red cherry jam
80g dried sour cherries
12 glacé cherries, halved

equipment
saucepan with tight-fitting lid

Begin by making the suet pastry. Place the flour, suet, baking powder, salt and sugar in a bowl and add the milk. Mix together with your hands and gradually add 80ml water. You may not need all the water, so add it a little at a time until you have a smooth, but not sticky, dough.

On a flour-dusted surface, roll out the pastry into a rectangle 30 x 20cm, slightly less than 1cm thick. Spread the cherry jam over the dough, leaving a margin of about 1cm between the jam and the edge of the pastry. Sprinkle the dried cherries and glacé cherry halves on top. Wet the edge of the dough with a little cold water and roll up from one of the narrow ends, enclosing the jam. Press the edges together to seal the jam inside.

Place a double sheet of baking parchment on a flat surface and fold a 5cm (total 10cm) crease in the centre. This will allow room for the pastry to expand during cooking. Place the suet roll in the centre and roll up in the paper. Tie up the ends of the pastry tightly with string. Wrap the parcel in cling film and tie another piece of string around it to act as a handle so that you can easily lift it out of the pan.

Place the pudding in a large saucepan of water and cover with a tight-fitting lid. Bring to the boil on the Boiling Plate and simmer for 30 minutes on the Simmering Plate, then transfer to the Simmering Oven and cook for a further $1^1/_2$ hours.

Remove the pudding from the water and allow to cool for a few minutes before opening. Do not leave wrapped in the cling film as it will shrink on cooling and make the pudding contract. Turn the pudding out onto a serving plate. Serve large slices with hot custard.

The pudding needs to be eaten straight away.

Baked amaretto nectarines with cherries

serves 8

When I worked in London, our company chef, Tony Carey, used to make the most delicious baked peaches. I begged him for the recipe and have continued to make them ever since. This is my version, made with nectarines and ripe cherries and is a perfect summertime dessert. If, like me, you are not overly fond of marzipan, don't be put off. The marzipan bakes into a soft, gooey paste with the amaretti biscuits and is utterly delicious.

PREPARATION: 25 MINUTES | BAKING: 50–65 MINUTES

4 ripe nectarines
120g amaretti biscuits
150g golden marzipan
60g butter, melted and kept warm
200g fresh cherries, stoned and stalks removed
100ml amaretto liqueur

equipment

Aga-proof roasting dish, large enough to hold the nectarine halves

Cut the nectarines in half and remove the stones. Place the nectarine halves cut side up in the roasting dish.

Crush the amaretti biscuits to small pieces using your hands. Cut small pieces of the marzipan and add to the biscuits. Pour the warm melted butter into the mixture and crush everything together with your hands.

Working with one nectarine half at a time, place a cherry in the hole left by the stone, then take a small handful of the amaretti mixture in your hand and press it over the top of the nectarine half where the other half of the nectarine would have been, forming a sphere; then return the nectarine to the dish. Repeat with the remaining nectarines. Add the leftover cherries to the dish and drizzle the amaretto on top.

Bake the nectarines in the Roasting Oven below a cold shelf (or in the Baking Oven) for 20 minutes, then transfer to the Simmering Oven for a further 30–45 minutes until the nectarines are soft.

Allow the nectarines to cool slightly before serving warm with crème fraîche or clotted cream.

The nectarines will store in the refrigerator for up to 2 days.

Raspberry pond pudding
serves 6

The classic Sussex pond pudding is one of my favourites. Although the suet pastry takes a while to steam, the results are worthwhile when you cut into the pudding to reveal the fruity syrup inside. Sussex pond pudding is traditionally made with lemons; this is my tangy version made with raspberries.

PREPARATION: 30 MINUTES | COOKING: APPROXIMATELY 4 HOURS

for the pastry
225g self-raising flour, sifted, plus extra for dusting
100g shredded suet
pinch of salt
80ml milk

for the filling
225g butter, chilled and cut into cubes
150g caster sugar
400g raspberries

equipment
1-litre pudding basin, greased; string; large Aga-
    proof saucepan with tight-fitting lid; palette knife

Begin by making the suet pastry. Place the flour, suet and salt in a bowl and add the milk. Mix together with your hands and gradually add 80ml water. You may not need all the water, so add it a little at a time until you have a smooth, but not sticky, dough.

On a flour-dusted surface, roll out the pastry into a circle 25/26cm in diameter and slightly less than 1cm thick. It is easiest to do this by rolling it slightly larger, then using a dinner plate as a template and cutting round it with a sharp knife. Next, cut away a quarter of the dough circle and set aside. This will be the cover for the pudding.

Wet the inside edges of the dough where the quarter has been cut away with a little cold water and place the dough into the pudding basin. The two cut-away edges of the dough should be pressed together so that the dough takes the shape of the basin. Press the dough into the bowl, ensuring that the straight opening edges are tightly joined.

On the flour-dusted surface, roll the remaining quarter of dough out into a circle the size of the top of the pudding basin; set this aside.

For the filling, layer a quarter of the sugar, a quarter of the butter and a quarter of the raspberries into the basin; repeat the layers until the pudding basin is filled. Wet the top edge of the dough in the basin with a little cold water and place the pastry lid on top. Press down tightly with your fingers to ensure that the filling is enclosed.

Take two layers of baking parchment and fold a pleat about 5cm wide (total 10cm) in the centre. Tie in place over the top of the pudding using string. The pleat will allow the pudding to expand as it cooks. Cover with a layer of foil and – again – tie in place with string. Tie a string handle over the top of the dish so that you can easily remove it when cooked.

Place the pudding in the saucepan and fill this with water up to the halfway point of the basin, taking care not to get any water into the pudding. Cover the pan with a tight-fitting lid and cook on the Boiling Plate for 40 minutes. Transfer to the Simmering Oven and cook for about $3^1/_2$ hours.

When you are ready to serve, remove the basin from the water and leave to cool slightly. Remove the foil and paper and slide a palette knife around the edge of the pudding to release it from the dish. Place a large plate on top of the pudding basin and carefully invert the pudding on to the plate. Take the golden pudding to the table and cut into it in front of your guests so that they see the pink raspberry syrup appear. Serve with clotted or double cream.

This pudding doesn't store well, so be sure to eat it straight away!

Sweet Things From the Aga

Chocolate peanut butter pie
serves 12

This is utterly indulgent and very, very rich, so small slices will suffice (although the pie is addictive and second, or even third helpings commonplace!) Packed with peanuts, chocolate, peanut sponge and caramel, this is a dessert with gusto and is certainly not for the faint-hearted or calorie conscious!

PREPARATION: 30 MINUTES | BAKING: 20–25 MINUTES | CHILLING: OVERNIGHT

for the crust
300g peanut biscuits
120g butter, melted

for the sponge
115g butter, softened
115g caster sugar
2 tablespoons peanut butter
2 eggs
115g self-raising flour, sifted

for the mousse
4 Snickers bars
250ml double cream
1 heaped tablespoon crunchy peanut butter
4 egg whites

to assemble
250ml double cream, whipped to stiff peaks
honey-roasted peanuts to sprinkle
30g plain chocolate, melted

equipment
23cm springform cake tin, greased and lined (see page 8), 20cm sandwich cake tin, greased and lined; piping bag fitted with a large star nozzle

Crush the peanut biscuits to fine crumbs in a food processor or place in a clean plastic bag and bash with a rolling pin. Stir the melted butter into the crumbs, then press into the base and sides of the springform tin firmly, using the back of a spoon. You need the case to come about 4–5 cm up the sides of the tin so that it will hold the mousse filling. Chill in the refrigerator for at least 1 hour.

For the sponge cake, cream together the butter, sugar and peanut butter. Whisk in the eggs, one at a time. Fold in the flour. Spoon the mixture into the sandwich tin and transfer to the bottom runners of the Roasting Oven below a cold shelf (or into the Baking Oven). Cook for about 20–25 minutes (turning the pan around halfway through this time) until a skewer inserted into the centre of the cake comes out clean and the cake springs back to your touch. Remove the cake from the oven and leave to cool completely.

For the mousse, chop the Snickers bars into small pieces and place in a saucepan with the double cream and peanut butter; heat on the Simmering Plate, stirring constantly, for about 3–5 minutes until the chocolate has melted and the peanut butter has blended with the cream into a smooth mixture with bits of peanut in it. Take care that the mixture does not burn. Leave to cool.

Whip the egg whites to stiff peaks and then fold in a third of the cooled peanut and chocolate mixture. Add the remaining mixture and fold in gently.

Cut the top and bottom crusts of the cake away; these can be discarded or frozen and used in making truffles, for example. Slice the remaining cake in half horizontally.

Pour one-third of the mousse into the chilled biscuit crust and top with one cake half. Pour in another third of the mousse and place the second cake on top. Cover the cake with the remaining mousse. Chill in the refrigerator overnight.

Place the whipped cream in a piping bag and pipe two rings of cream stars around the edge of the cake. Sprinkle the peanuts on top and drizzle with thin lines of chocolate using a fork. Store in the refrigerator until ready to serve.

This dessert will keep, refrigerated, for up to 3 days. Note that it is not suitable for pregnant women, as it contains raw egg whites.

Cookie dough apple pie
serves 8

Apple pie is one of my favourite desserts, bursting with cinnamon and sugar. In place of the classic pastry crust, this recipe has an oatmeal cinnamon cookie dough topping which bakes on top of the apples to make a delicious crust. I prefer large apple quarters in my apple pie (this is the way my American sister-in-law, Amy, makes it); but if you prefer, or are short of time, you can slice the apples more thinly and reduce the cooking time for the apples.

PREPARATION: 30 MINUTES | BAKING: 50–70 MINUTES

for the apple filling
12 eating apples, peeled, cut into quarters and cored
50g caster sugar
100g sultanas
2 teaspoons ground cinnamon

for the cookie dough topping
350g self-raising flour
1/2 teaspoon bicarbonate of soda
1 teaspoon ground cinnamon
1 egg
115g butter
100g caster sugar
2 tablespoons golden syrup
80g porridge oats

equipment
Aga-proof baking dish approximately 25cm in diameter

Place the apple quarters in the baking dish with the sugar, sultanas, cinnamon and 100ml water. Cover the dish with a sheet of kitchen foil and bake in the centre of the Roasting Oven for about 30–40 minutes until the apples are soft enough to be cut through easily with a knife. If the apples start to brown, cover with a cold shelf. Remove from the oven and cool while you prepare the topping.

For the cookie dough topping, sift the flour, bicarbonate of soda and cinnamon together in a large mixing bowl. Beat the egg and whisk into the flour.

Heat the butter, sugar and syrup in a saucepan on the Boiling Plate until the butter has melted. Cool slightly, then stir the syrup mixture into the oats and mix until you have a sticky dough.

Place spoonfuls of the cookie dough mixture evenly over the top of the baked apples, spreading it out with a knife or spatula. Return the pie to the Roasting Oven and bake for 20–30 minutes until the topping is golden brown, covering with a cold shelf if the topping starts to brown too much (or transfer to the Baking Oven, if appropriate).

Serve the pie warm with double cream or custard.

The pie will keep in the refrigerator for up to 2 days.

Rhubarb and ginger pavlova
serves 8

Pavlova is one of the best desserts to make in the Aga, as the Simmering Oven is the perfect temperature for baking meringues. I always use silicone mats for baking meringues on, so that they don't stick, but you can use baking parchment if you do not have a silicone mat. Pavlova is commonly served with strawberries or raspberries, but I've given this classic my own twist with a delicately ginger-scented meringue and oven-poached rhubarb – especially good when rhubarb is first in season.

PREPARATION: 30 MINUTES | COOKING: 1^1/$_2$ HOURS

for the meringue
4 egg whites
225g caster sugar
2 teaspoons ground ginger, sifted

for the rhubarb compote
100g caster sugar
3cm piece of ginger root, peeled and thinly
    sliced
450g pink rhubarb, trimmed

for the topping
200ml crème fraîche
200ml soured cream

equipment
large baking tray lined with a silicone mat;
    piping bag fitted with a large round nozzle

For the meringue, whisk the egg whites to stiff peaks in a large bowl. While still whisking, add the caster sugar, one tablespoonful at a time. The meringue should be glossy and hold a peak when you lift the beaters. Sprinkle the ginger over the top of the meringue and fold through gently.

Spoon the meringue on to the centre of the silicone mat and spread out gently, using a spatula, into a disc about 22cm in diameter. Using the spatula, make a well in the centre and pull the outside meringue into decorative swirls and peaks.

Slide the tray onto the bottom runners of the Simmering Oven and bake for 1–1^1/$_4$ hours until the meringue is crisp and slightly golden,

turning the tray halfway through this time to ensure even cooking. Remove from the oven and leave to cool.

To prepare the rhubarb, place the sugar and sliced ginger in a saucepan with 180ml water and simmer until you have a thin syrup.

Chop the rhubarb into long pieces and place in a small roasting pan. Pour the ginger syrup and ginger slices over the rhubarb and bake in the Roasting Oven for 10–15 minutes until the rhubarb is just soft. Check halfway through the cooking time and turn the pan if the rhubarb is starting to cook more on one side than on the other. When the rhubarb is soft, remove it from the oven and leave to cool completely.

When you are ready to serve, whisk together the crème fraîche and soured cream. Place the meringue carefully on a serving plate and top with the cream mixture.

Drain the rhubarb (reserving the syrup) and remove the ginger, then spoon the rhubarb over the cream; drizzle with a little of the ginger syrup.

Store the pavlova in the refrigerator if you are not eating it straight away. The meringue without the topping will keep for at least a week stored in an airtight container. Once covered with the cream and rhubarb, it will keep for up to 2 days in the refrigerator; but it is best eaten on the day it is made.

Blackcurrant and lemon cheesecake
serves 12

Baked cheesecake is a classic American dessert. It is often flavoured simply with vanilla; this is my version, embellished with lemon and blackcurrants, although you can substitute blueberries for the blackcurrants if you prefer. This cheesecake makes an ideal dessert when you are entertaining a group of friends, as it can be prepared the day before and stored in the refrigerator until you are ready to serve it. Cheesecakes are quite temperature sensitive, and baking in a water bath will help ensure even cooking.

PREPARATION: 20 MINUTES | BAKING: APPROXIMATELY 1^1/$_2$ HOURS| CHILLING: 3 HOURS

for the base
300g digestive biscuits
125g butter, melted

for the filling
150g blackcurrants, fresh or, if tinned, drained
600ml crème fraîche
600g cream cheese
4 eggs
400g condensed milk
2 tablespoons plain flour, sifted
juice and zest of 2 lemons

equipment
23cm springform cake tin, greased and lined
(see page 8); large Aga roasting pan

Note: It's important to ensure that the sides of your springform tin fit tightly; test the tin for possible leaks by putting some water into it before using it

Crush the biscuits to fine crumbs in a food processor or place them in a clean plastic bag and bash with a rolling pin. Stir in the melted butter, then press firmly into the base of the tin using the back of a spoon. You want the biscuit mix to come about 4–5cm up the sides of the tin to hold the cheesecake filling.

Wrap the tin carefully in heatproof cling film, bringing the film up the sides so that it ends at the top edge (folding it where necessary). Place the tin in a large roasting pan and fill the pan with water up to the halfway point on the tin.

If using fresh blackcurrants (or blueberries), place them in a saucepan with 100ml of water and simmer on the Boiling Plate for a few minutes until just soft. Drain and leave to cool.

For the filling, whisk together the crème fraîche, cream cheese, eggs, condensed milk, flour, and juice and zest of the lemons. Pour the mixture into the biscuit case. Sprinkle the blackcurrants over the top of the cheesecake.

Transfer the water bath to the Roasting Oven for 30 minutes, turning the cheesecake halfway through baking and covering it with a cold shelf if it starts to brown too much. Transfer to the Simmering Oven and bake for a further 1 hour until the cheesecake is set but still has slight wobble in the centre.

Remove the cheesecake from the water bath and slide a palette knife around the edge of the tin to ensure that the cheesecake does not stick to the sides. The cheesecake will shrink as it cools, and doing this will prevent it from cracking on top. Leave it to cool, then transfer to the refrigerator to chill for at least 3 hours or preferably overnight.

Serve the cheesecake with extra berries and pouring cream if you wish.

This cheesecake mixture will store in the refrigerator, covered, for up to 3 days.

Sweet Things From the Aga

Peach and plum crumble
serves 6-8

Everyone loves a good crumble. When ripe summer fruits are in season, this is the perfect crumble to make, bursting with peaches and plum, enhanced with a drizzle of almond liqueur and a crunchy nut topping. If serving to children, you can replace the alcohol with water if you wish.

PREPARATION: 20 MINUTES | COOKING: ABOUT 40–50 MINUTES

for the fruit filling
500g red plums, stoned and cut into slices
4 ripe peaches, stoned and cut into slices
60g caster sugar
60ml amaretto liqueur

for the crumble topping
170g self-raising flour
1 teaspoon baking powder
85g ground almonds
125g butter, chilled and cut into cubes
60g dark muscovado sugar
60g caster sugar
30g flaked almonds

equipment
25cm Aga-proof baking dish, greased

Place the plums and peaches in the baking dish; sprinkle with the caster sugar and spoon the amaretto over them. Mix together so that all the fruit is coated with the amaretto and sugar. Bake in the Roasting Oven for about 10 minutes, until the fruit starts to soften.

For the crumble topping, sift the flour and baking powder into a bowl. Add the ground almonds and mix with the flour. Rub the chilled butter into the flour mixture with your fingertips until it resembles breadcrumbs. Stir in the muscovado sugar, caster sugar and flaked almonds.

Sprinkle the crumble in a thick layer over the top of the fruit. Bake for about 30–40 minutes in the Roasting Oven below a cold shelf (or in the Baking Oven) until the fruit juices start to bubble up through the crumble topping and the topping is golden-brown.

Transfer the crumble to the Simmering Oven and keep it warm until you are ready to serve. For an extra-special treat, serve the crumble with custard or clotted cream.

The crumble can be stored in the refrigerator for up to 3 days and can be frozen for up to 1 month.

Baked Alaskas

serves 4

For me, baked Alaska always brings back childhood memories of wonderful birthday parties. This delicious dessert seems to be having a resurgence of late and is often served in trendy retro restaurants. Quite frankly it should never have gone away! I never cease to be amazed at the ice cream staying frozen even though it has been baked in a hot oven. The meringue is Italian meringue, which is cooked by adding hot sugar syrup to the egg whites, so that only a short amount of cooking is required to brown the meringue. In this modern twist on the classic recipe, these mini Alaskas are filled with chocolate mint ice cream and served with an indulgent chocolate peppermint sauce, making it the perfect dessert for a sophisticated dinner party. You need to serve them immediately to ensure that your guests have the true 'hot-and-cold' Alaska experience, as the ice cream melts quickly.

PREPARATION: 25 MINUTES | BAKING: 25–30 MINUTES

for the cake bases
115g butter, softened
115g caster sugar
2 eggs
85g self-raising flour, sifted
30g cocoa, sifted
100g white chocolate chips

for the sauce
300ml double cream
100g After Eight (or similar dark chocolate) mints

for the meringue
400g caster sugar
4 large egg whites

for the filling
800ml mint chocolate chip ice cream

equipment
20cm sandwich cake tin, greased and lined (see page 8); 8cm round cutter; sugar thermometer; Aga-proof serving plates; chef's blowtorch (optional)

Begin by preparing your ice cream. Line a small tea cup with a sheet of clingfilm. Fill with the ice cream, then pull the clingfilm tightly over the top of the ice cream and remove it from the cup. Place in the freezer. Repeat this process 3 more times and store the 4 wrapped balls of ice cream in the the freezer until needed.

In a mixing bowl, cream together the butter and sugar, using a mixer or hand whisk, until light and fluffy. Add the eggs one at a time, whisking after each egg is added. Sift in the flour and cocoa, add the chocolate chips and fold through gently with a spatula to incorporate.

Spoon the cake batter into the prepared cake tin and bake on the bottom runners of the Roasting Oven below a cold shelf for 20–25 minutes (or in the Baking Oven), turning the pan halfway through cooking to ensure even browning. The cake is ready when it springs back to your touch and a skewer inserted into the centre comes out clean. Turn the cake out on to a rack and leave it to cool.

While the cake is cooling, prepare the chocolate mint sauce. Place the double cream and mints in a saucepan on the Simmering Plate and simmer until the mints have melted and you have a smooth, glossy chocolate sauce. Leave the sauce on top of the Aga to keep warm until serving. (Or, if you have made it ahead of time, remove from the heat and then reheat just before you are ready to serve.)

To prepare the meringue, add the caster sugar to 120ml of water in a saucepan and simmer it on the Boiling Plate until the sugar has dissolved, then bring it to the boil. Using a sugar thermometer to measure, bring the syrup to 119°C, the soft ball stage. Remove from the heat and leave on top of the Aga.

Whisk the egg whites to stiff peaks. Check the temperature of the sugar syrup and reheat to 119°C if necessary, then slowly add the syrup to

the egg whites in a fine drizzle, whisking constantly as you pour it in. This is best done with a stand mixer; if using a hand mixer, have someone else pour in the hot sugar syrup. Whisk the meringue for about 10–15 minutes. Leave until you are ready to serve.

Because you are working with ice cream, you need to have all of your equipment prepared in advance and be ready to serve immediately once the meringue is caramelised. Using the cutter, cut out 4 rounds of cake and place one in the centre of each plate. Remove the cling film from the ice cream shapes and place one on each cake. Working quickly, cover the ice cream and

cake with meringue and swirl into peaks using a spatula knife. Toast the outside of the meringue with the blowtorch until lightly golden-brown. You can also toast the meringue on the bottom runners of the Roasting Oven with the door open. Using oven gloves, turn the Alaskas once or twice to ensure that they are browned evenly. Depending on the temperature of your oven, it should take around 3–5 minutes for the Alaskas to turn a golden caramel colour. (Make sure you use heatproof plates.)

Serve the baked Alaskas immediately with the hot chocolate mint sauce.

Puddings, Tarts & Delicious Desserts

Baked gingerbread apples
serves 6

In the autumn, when the apple trees in my garden are laden, I love to make baked apples. They may be an old-fashioned dessert, but they are quick and easy to prepare and are a perfect Aga dish which can be left cooking slowly in the Simmering Oven until you are ready to serve. Baked apples are ideal for Bonfire Night and Halloween parties, when you need something warm and comforting to eat while standing outdoors (usually in the rain!). Traditionally, they are filled only with syrup and sultanas, but I have added a spicy ginger kick to mine – with gingerbread crumbs and stem ginger. I used red as well as green apples here, just for variety of colour, but green apples on their own will do nicely.

PREPARATION: 10 MINUTES | BAKING: APPROXIMATELY 1½ HOURS

6 large cooking apples
2 balls of stem ginger preserved in syrup
100g gingerbread (such as Jamaican ginger cake), crumbled
60g raisins or sultanas
6 tablespoon golden syrup

equipment
apple corer; roasting pan or Aga-proof dish large enough to hold the apples

Using a sharp knife, score a thin line horizontally around the centre of each apple; this will prevent the skins from splitting during cooking. Remove the cores using the apple corer to make a large hole in the middle of each apple (I usually remove three plugs with the apple corer to make this larger). Place the apples in a roasting pan or Aga-proof dish.

Finely chop the preserved stem ginger, then mix this together with the gingerbread crumbs and raisins or sultanas. Fill each apple with the ginger mixture. Spoon the golden syrup over the apples and add 6 tablespoons of water to the dish.

Bake in the Roasting Oven beneath a cold shelf (or in the Baking Oven) for 20–30 minutes, then transfer to the Simmering Oven and slow cook for a further 1 hour until the apples are soft. You can keep the apples warm in the simmering oven for a few further hours if you wish. Serve each apple with a drizzle of the cooking syrup and some cream or custard if you wish. For an extra treat, serve them with golden custard to which you've added a little of the syrup from the preserved stem ginger.

These apples are best eaten on the day they are made, but can be kept in the refrigerator and reheated the following day.